Back Lane Wineries
OF NEW YORK STATE

BY NISH GERA

PHOTOS BY PETER VERBRUGGHE

WITH TILAR J. MAZZEO

Published by Bayshore Press, New York, NY

©2017 Bayshore Press

Text ©2017 Nish Gera

Photos ©2017 Peter Verbrugghe

Design: Raphael G. A. Batista

bayshorepress@gmail.com

ISBN: 978-1-63337-194-1

Backlane Wineries of New York State / by Nish Gera; photos by Peter Verbrugghe, with Tilar J. Mazzeo

TABLE OF CONTENTS

SORRY
NO
BUSES
OR
LIMOS

ridge

INTRODUCTION

THE FACT THAT NEW YORK STATE IS A PLACE OF BOUNTY IS no secret. That was discovered more than 10,000 years ago by the first Native American tribes to make this region their home, and today many of the state's lakes and towns bear the names of the people who flourished here, or bear traces of their languages: Adirondack, Niagara, Erie, Keuka, Seneca, and, of course, Manhattan. Today, as the New York State wine industry invents and reinvents itself in ways that did not seem possible just a few decades ago, that history and bounty—and the history and bounty of everything that came after—are all part of its story of dynamism and tradition.

Grapevines grow wild across North America. In fact, nowhere in the world boasts more indigenous grape species than this continent. The Native American people were the first to enjoy their fruits, but when European settlers arrived they brought with them a taste for the Vitis vinifera grapevines of the Old World, and by the middle of the nineteenth century, industrious New Yorkers were already creating new grape varietals that

hybridized the local wild grapes with cuttings from Europe. Those hybridizations, alongside classic vinifera species, are still at the heart of the New York State wine industry.

It was here—in New York State and not in California—that the first bonded winery in the United States, the Pleasant Valley Wine Company in Hammondsport, was founded. New York State also boasts America's oldest continuously operating winery, the Brotherhood Winery in the Hudson Valley. For generations, the wine industry here, like the wine industry in California, struggled to produce excellent quality wines. And, as with California, this wine region only began to find its sweet spot in the later part of the twentieth century. That means that the story of the rise of New York State wine is unfolding now. Visiting the region is a rare chance to watch this kind of history in the making. Today, the state is making world-class wine. In the span of a decade, it has emerged as a wine region that is being taken seriously by wine lovers, writers, and connoisseurs, and it is no longer unusual to find news items singing the praises of New York State wines in trade journals and wine magazines. The wines made from the Riesling plantings in the region are winning top prizes in international competitions and its Burgundy-style Chardonnays are being served in top New York City restaurants, though New York State's "Judgment of Paris" is still ahead of it. What this all means is that there is still

time to make your own discoveries on the "back lanes" of New York State's wine country.

For all its recent success, the story of New York wine is not an easy one. It was not inevitable that a great wine region would be born in this climate. The fact that it has been is largely down to the courage, enterprise, and faith of a remarkably small group of people who first believed that world-class wine could be made here, in spite of the unpredictable and extreme climate. The wide variation in weather and growing conditions, however, is part of what gives the wines of New York State their more distinctive qualities and what makes each new vintage its own creature and its own celebration. When you hear wine-makers in the Finger Lakes proudly talk about "vintage variation" it is this unique set of circumstances and the constant struggle to make great wine in a marginal climate that they are talking about.

It's also worth saying a bit more at the outset about those native grape varietals. Unless you are an experienced wine aficionado, the ins-and-outs of the hybridization of grape species are probably new territory, but those hybridizations are key to understanding and appreciating much of what makes the wines of New York State special. Most commercially grown wine grapes around the world, and especially in Europe, belong to a species

of grape called *Vitis vinifera*. Human cultures have grown this species of grape since the Neolithic period, and today there are a few thousand varieties of *Vitis vinifera*. Only a few, however, are of interest to most wine drinkers and winemakers. Those are the names you recognize from your favorite wine bottle: Cabernet Sauvignon, Cabernet Franc, Chardonnay, and Pinot Noir, for example.

In New York State, though, *Vitis vinifera* was rarely grown before the 1960s. It was widely believed that the grape, which thrives in sunny places like France and Spain and in Mediterranean climates, would not survive the harsh winters of the northeast, where deep freezes and even deeper snows are common. Most of the grapes indigenous to this region belonged, instead, to the hardier *Vitis labrusca* species of grape, which is native to the Eastern United States and includes varietals such as Concord and Catawba.

This all changed when a Ukrainian named Konstantin Frank arrived in the Finger Lakes area of New York in the 1950s. This new immigrant made a claim that led some people to conclude that he was crazy: he claimed that not only would *vinifera* grow here, but he insisted that it would thrive. Specifically, he believed that it was vineyard land ideally suited for the cool-climate varietal Riesling, which had long made exceptional wines in Germany and Austria. Konstantin Frank was ridiculed but determined, and he set out to show that New York State could make fine wine from the noble *vinifera* grape varieties. And he did. Today, wine growers in the state are making world-class

Riesling and Chardonnay white wines and excellent red wines from the Cabernet Franc, Cabernet Sauvignon, and Pinot Noir varietals.

The state also has significant plantings of some more unusual grape varietals whose names might not be quite so familiar. These are the so-called French-American hybrids, grape species that cross various cool-climate *vinifera* varietals with each other and with some of the best Native American species, in order to develop modern vines capable of thriving in the cold-climate regions of the wine world. These are grape varietals like Cayuga or the sparkling-wine producer Aurore, and, while they are not "noble" species, they produce excellent quality wines in the hands of a talented winemaker.

There has been nothing short of a revolution in New York State winemaking since the 1970s, and the quality and variety only continues to rise. That rise has already been meteoric. Not restricted by centuries-old traditions and techniques but often benefiting from generations of experience, and less encumbered by the regulations that control winemaking in Europe, the winemakers here are free to experiment with styles and vineyard-management techniques, making unique and innovative expressions of cool-climate varietals. And the world is catching on. New York State today ranks third in the United

States' wine production by volume, after only California and Washington State. The state has on the order of 350 wineries in operation, and over five million people visit these wineries every year. Perhaps this is the year that you will be one of them.

New York State has four major wine-growing regions or AVAs (American Viticultural Areas): the Finger Lakes AVA, the Long Island AVA, the Hudson Valley AVA and the Lake Erie AVA. The Finger Lakes and Long Island AVAs are getting most of the

professional attention because of their recent focus on *vinifera* varietals and the larger number of wineries here. Because these AVAs circumscribe geographical areas, we have organized this guide around these areas and suggest that you organize your tasting adventures in the same fashion. Where you go depends on your tasting preferences. The Hudson Valley and Lake Erie are where French-American hybrids and the most truly "native" New York State wines are still being crafted.

WINE TASTING ESSENTIALS

WINE TASTING SHOULD BE FUN. THAT SHOULD BE STATing the obvious. But for a long time, the professional world of wine has emphasized the technical over the gustatory and that has made wine seem obscure and daunting for a variety of reasons. Fortunately, that is now changing quickly. Many New York State winemakers, especially, are finding new ways of thinking and talking about their wines. These are wine industry experts who enjoy sharing their knowledge and stories with beginners and experts alike, and you don't have to be an expert in the New York State wine country to enter the conversation. In fact, the warmest welcome here is generally reserved for the passionate amateur.

There are a few things to keep in mind when you embark on your tasting adventures, however, to make sure you are fully able to immerse yourself in the wine-tasting experience. If you're already a wine expert, this is a section you might wish

to skip. But if you're new to the wine-appreciation game, just a couple of pro-tips will get you off and running in the right direction. The three S's of wine tasting usually suffice—swirl, sniff and sip.

Swirl: Wine is much more about aroma than about taste. The reason is simple: the human nose can recognize thousands of different aromas, but we experience only six different tastes. Wine tasting is about learning to recognize some of the marvelous ways those six tastes and thousands of aromas intermingle and unfold in the time of our experience.

These aromas, however, are what winemakers sometimes call "volatile aromatics." Volatile means they are constantly being released, changing and interacting. And you can help them to release and interact more quickly. Just hold your glass by the stem—the temperature of your hand can change the temperature of the wine fairly quickly, and besides greasy fingerprints are not elegant—and give it a good swirl. This is done to aerate the wine so it can release its aromas. Wine glasses are shaped the way they are to concentrate these aromas. Most of us swirl by moving the glass around in circles while it is still on a countertop or table knowing that discretion is the better part of valor. But, if you are feeling more adventurous or practiced, you can always attempt the mid-air swirl of experts.

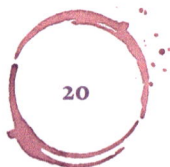

SNIFF: Next, take a long, slow sniff by placing your nose above the bowl of the glass. The important thing here, unless you are in a blind-tasting contest or preparing for a sommelier exam, is not to be able to describe every aroma in the glass. What you are simply trying to do is appreciate the unique sensory experience that makes *this* wine special. You can swirl again and take a deeper sniff by tilting the glass a little and burying your nose a bit closer to the glass. Pros often move from nostril to nostril, as well, with a gentle tilt of the head that also manages to look knowing. Rotating nostrils, in fact, does improve your ability to appreciate aromas. This time, you might experience a different set of aromas. As with perfume, wine aromas have lighter notes and heavier notes, as well as notes that evolve over the time that it takes for a wine to unfold. That's part of the reason why wine tasting is best enjoyed as a leisurely experience.

SIP: When you're ready, take a sip of the wine and quietly swish it around in your mouth for a moment. Your fellow wine tasters implore you not to slurp or gargle. We are trying to have an aesthetic moment here. Different parts of your tongue have taste buds that register different tastes, and it is important that all of the areas get to touch the wine. At this point, you can also try to inhale some air into your mouth while holding the wine at the back of your mouth if you want. This aspirates the wine and releases flavors and aromas even further. Here, you might hear

from your neighbors a bit of odd inhaling and heavy breathing, but rest assured this is *de rigueur* at many wine tastings.

After you sip the wine, there are no rules about whether to spit or swallow, except for the obvious advice that drinking and driving is both dangerous and expensive. All wineries provide spit buckets, and there is nothing in the least bit rude about using them. If you're out for a full day of tasting and are deciding on purchases for your home "cellar," spitting is the only way to focus on what you are buying. Remember, whatever you decide, all those little sips can add up very quickly, and even when you are spitting you are still absorbing some alcohol. There is, of course, a time of the day where you just want to settle down on that outdoor patio overlooking the vineyard with that chilled bottle of Riesling and some cheese. This experience is always highly recommended. But so is having a designated driver.

The winemakers you visit will generally set out the order in which you taste, but you will quickly notice a method to their collective madness. Wine tasting is usually done starting with the lightest bodied whites and moving on to the fullest bodied reds, with the concentrated dessert wines, red or white, tasted at the end. However, both your palate and your nose can get fatigued after tasting several wines, even in a single flight,

despite the careful ordering. With practice, you will know when that happens, and the best thing to do is to take a bit of palate cleanser, usually either a piece of bread or crackers.

When planning a day of wine tasting, a few other considerations will help you make the most of your experience. First, consider starting early. Most wineries open at 10 or 11 a.m., and tasting rooms generally get busier in the afternoon. In the summers, especially, things can get crowded on the tasting trail. If you're traveling in the low season, by the same token, consider making a few reservations. Most tasting rooms are open to the public without reservations on the weekends and in the summer months, but winemakers are generally delighted to welcome you in the winter and on weekdays, and you'll often get a chance to meet the proprietor one-on-one when things are quieter. But winter is also pruning season in the vineyard, and there's often a lot of cellar work going on behind the scenes. You may need to let a winemaker know so they can plan to welcome you.

Generally, two or three tasting appointments in a day are plenty, especially if you are planning to take your time and enjoy the experience. We also recommend making time for a leisurely lunch somewhere. The great thing about the New York State wine country is that there are many options for delicious "slow-food" and "farm-to-table" experiences. Both the Finger Lakes and the North Fork region, especially, have a wide range of

options for lunch, and we recommend some of our favorites in this guide.

There is also the delicate matter of wine tasting and the etiquette of wine buying. You are never under any obligation to purchase wine, and it is common for tasting rooms to charge a modest fee in order to offset the costs of the wine that they are pouring. If you've paid the tasting fee there is nothing rude about not purchasing, although many wineries will waive the tasting fee if you buy even a single bottle. But if you like the wine, and especially if the winemaker is pouring the wine without charging a tasting fee, the polite thing to do is to buy a bottle or two, especially if a winemaker has also taken time from

his or her busy day or from cellar work in order to give you a great experience. It's the best compliment you can give a small proprietor, and, besides, back at home there are few experiences more pleasurable than sharing a bottle of wine with friends that you brought back from your travels.

If you do buy, and especially if you plan to make enough purchases to stock your home wine cellar, keep in mind that wines don't fare well if they are kept in hot cars for long periods. If you're visiting in the summer, try to park in the shade or consider picking up (or packing) a cooler. You can pick up inexpensive Styrofoam coolers for a few dollars in most drugstores on the road if you didn't think ahead.

If you're planning to take things home and that journey involves airline travel, don't despair either. Some wineries sell, for a modest fee, larger boxes especially designed for sending wine as checked luggage if you want to send a case home, and nearly any winery you visit will help you pack your purchases in one of the standard case boxes, which are also perfectly acceptable for airline travel. Wine bottles are generally very sturdy, and in years of sending wines as checked luggage only rarely have we lost a bottle. If you are purchasing just a bottle or two, you can also tuck them inside a suitcase. Just remember to pad them well, and we recommend, for red wines especially, wrapping the bottles in a plastic bag just in case there is any leakage. Another option, of course, is to take your wine boxes to a private shipping outlet such as FedEx or UPS and to have the case shipped home ahead of you. It generally costs $50-75 to send a case of wine home, though the actual price will naturally depend on the destination. Either way, you will want to check your state's (or country's) wine importation requirements, to make sure you understand any duties. However, within the United States transporting wine home is generally quite easily accomplished.

THE
Finger
Lakes

TO VISIT THE FINGER LAKES IS TO TAKE A WALK THROUGH geologic time. Some 10,000 years ago, most of New York State was covered in ice and glaciers. At the end of the last ice age, as temperatures warmed, those glaciers slowly but violently retreated northward. In their wake, the cut eroded the land beneath, carving deep, irregular scars into the landscape, which then filled with rain and melting ice-water. Some of these became the Finger Lakes of New York State and some of them became the spectacular gorges and, eventually, waterfalls for which this area is rightly famous. The two longest of these lakes, Seneca and Cayuga, are among the deepest lakes any-where in the United States, with bottoms that rest well below sea level.

As with many of the world's great wine regions, this geography is part of what makes the Finger Lakes so well suited for the production of fine vintages. The water of the lakes both modu-lates the temperatures of the vineyards planted near them and reflects back onto the land a surprising amount of sunlight. To immerse oneself in the wine culture of the Finger Lakes region is to feel the excitement of an area that is relatively young—both in terms of geology and viticulture—but already producing some fine wines that are only getting better with each vintage.

The Finger Lakes AVA is New York's largest wine producing region, and most of its vineyards and wineries are located on the shores of Seneca, Keuka, and Cayuga lakes. The lakes retain much-needed summer heat well into the autumn and provide a warming and protective influence to the vines during the cold and generally harsh New York State winters.

The winters might be cold, but this in itself is no impediment to great winemaking. The Finger Lakes area is roughly at the same latitude as Germany's Mosel region and is often compared to this cool-climate and famous German winemaking region. It is no surprise that both regions are renowned for producing exceptional Riesling wines, though the Finger Lakes AVA is also increasingly known for the quality of white-wine varietals such as Gewurztraminer, Pinot Blanc, Sauvignon Blanc, and Chardonnay. The fact that the region also produces some fine quality red wines, including award-winning Cabernet Franc wines, is still very much a well-kept secret.

Given the length of Seneca, Cayuga, and Keuka Lakes and the absence of any bridges across them, the best way to plan a day of wine tasting is to pick a "side" and to stick to it. The drive from Watkins Glen, on the southern tip of Seneca Lake, to the town of Geneva, on the northern tip, for example, is about forty miles and takes under an hour to drive. But it should

take a guided
VINEYARD TOUR

$5 - tour only
OR
$8 - combined with a tasting
15yrs old & under are FREE

45 minute walking tour through the *vineyard*

LEARN ABOUT WINEMAKING IN THE FLX!

Last tour out @ 4 PM

EVERY TOUR departs the tasting room at the TOP of the HOUR

* weather permitting *

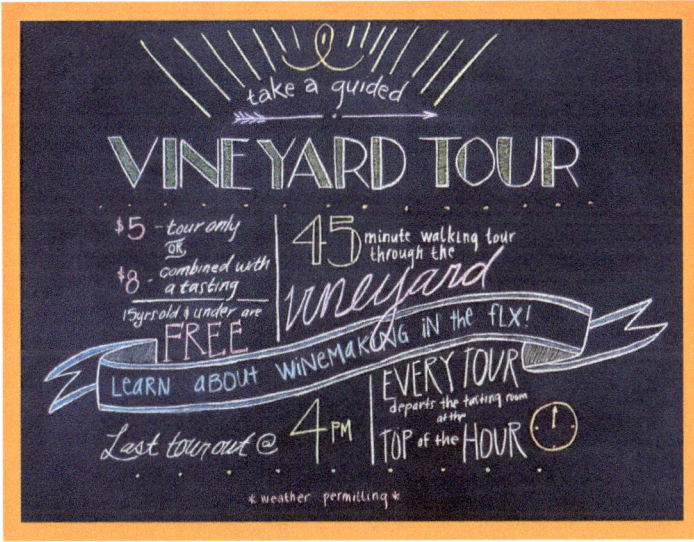

take you much longer than that if you're doing it right—and by "right" we mean wine tasting. Likewise, Ithaca, on the southern tip of Cayuga Lake, and Seneca Falls, on the northern tip, are about the same distance apart, and this makes for another convenient itinerary for a day trip. Any of these four cities can also serve as the perfect base for staying overnight at one of many quaint B&Bs and hotels. Ithaca, of course, is home to Cornell University, and many of the winemakers and viticulturists in the area have links to this institution and its world-famous viticulture program. Keuka Lake, the westernmost in this trio of lakes, is smaller and has fewer amenities, but it also has the

most panoramic views of all, and in some senses, it is the historic heart of the New York State wine country. Keuka, after all, is where the legendary Dr. Konstantin Frank winery is located, founded by and named after the man who pioneered *Vitis vinifera* cultivation in the region.

Seneca Lake

Legend:
- ● Winery
- ■ Eatery
- ★ Byways & Distractions

20

Geneva On The Lake

Billsboro Winery

96

Fox Run Vineyards

Red Tail Ridge Winery

Anthony Road Wine Company

Kemmeter Wines

94A

Seneca Lake

14

94A

96

Suzanne

Silver Thread Vineyard

King's Garden Vineyards

Hermann J. Wiemer Vineyard

Dano's Heuriger On Seneca

Shalestone Vineyards

14A

F.L.X. Wienery

414

Leidenfrost Vineyards

Hector Wine Company

Bloomer Creek Vineyard

Atwater Estate Vineyard

Damiani Wine Cellars

79

226

14A

Barnstormer Winery

★ Hector Falls

Seneca Lake

THE SENECA LAKE WINE TRAIL IS ONE OF NEW YORK STATE'S most active and renowned tasting areas. The first winery in this area dates back to the 1860s, when the Seneca Lake Grape Wine Company opened its doors on the western banks. By the 1980s, there were enough producers in the region to establish a formal "wine trail" for intrepid tourists and gastronomic adventurers keen to taste-test some of the region's early productions in white-wine varietals. Today, Seneca Lake, like much of New York State's wine country, is quickly becoming known for the quality of the red wines it also produces. There was a time when people said you couldn't make great red wines in this cool climate. The thirty-odd producers on the Seneca Lake wine trail are changing that perception, and the region's Cabernet Franc and Merlot offerings are especially celebrated by wine-industry insiders. The region is also crafting award-winning Pinot Noir, Pinot Gris, Cabernet Sauvignon, Riesling, and Chardonnay wines, among other varietals.

DAMIANI WINE CELLARS

4704 NY State Route 414, Burdett
607.546.5557
www.damianiwinecellars.com

The Damiani Wine Cellars' vineyards are located in what the locals call "The Seneca Lake Banana Belt." This is the nine-mile stretch that runs from Burdett to Valois on the eastern shore of the lake. The lake is deepest here, and the airflow from the water makes this the warmest stretch of the lake. Fruit for Damiani's wines comes from three vineyards—those at Damiani and vineyards planted at the Davis and Sunrise Hill estates but managed and carefully tended to by the three co-owners of Damiani Cellars.

Perched on a small hill on the east side of Route 414 in Burdett, the tasting room here also has striking view of Seneca Lake. And there's something else special about Damiani: they were the first winery in the region to get a 90-point rating from *Wine Spectator* for a red wine, for their 2010 Reserve Cabernet Sauvignon. They also produce must-try Meritage and Syrah wines and a Sauvignon Blanc that's interesting for its unconventional palate profile. If you find yourself in the New York State wine country on a weekend, there is live music Thursday through Saturday and a bocce court open on Sundays.

PLEASE
NO SMOKING

ATWATER ESTATE VINEYARDS

5055 NY State Route 414, Burdett
607.546.8463
www.atwatervineyards.com

The Atwater vineyards are located on the southeastern slopes of Seneca Lake and have a long and rich history. As early as the 1900s, this bit of land was already planted with native grape variet- ies such as Concord and Catawba, and early settlers recognized this "banana belt" parcel from the start as a location ideally suited for vineyard production. After changing hands several times over the course of the century, local entrepreneur Ted Marks bought the vine- yards and opened the doors of the winery in 2000. Since then, Ted has been reimagining the vineyard and helping to reshape New York State winemaking in the process. The more rustic na- tive-grape varietals have been increasingly replaced with *vinif- era* acreage, and today about 70% of the plantings are "noble." The Rieslings and Cabernet Francs are particular standouts and

have earned accolades from venues such as the *Wine Spectator*. The Rosé is also a perennial summer favorite.

If you're looking for a romantic dining experience in the vineyard, Atwater does outdoor summer dining on warm evenings among the grape vines. Their "Vineyard Table" program pairs Atwater wines with dishes prepared by the talented chef from the nearby Red Dove Tavern. Check their website or call the winery for details. Most wines in the $15 to $30 range; case production is around 7,000.

BLOOMER CREEK VINEYARD

5301 NY State Route 414, Hector
607.546.5027
www.bloomercreek.com

Kim Engle was a young student at Cornell University in the late 1970s when he found himself pruning grapes in a vineyard overlooking Cayuga Lake. Working with his hands in the vineyards and relishing the wine-country life, he realized that he might just have discovered his life's passion. After a season in the Alto Adige region of Northern Italy, he was no longer wondering. Kim was hooked and decided to return to the Cayuga region. He started buying land and planting grapes, learning the art of winemaking as he went along.

Bloomer Creek Vineyard was established in 1999 on ten acres of land. In 2012, Kim and his partner Debra added another vineyard, which had been abandoned and was located on the east side of Seneca Lake.

Kim definitely likes to take risks when making his wines, and Bloomer Creek was an early cult winery among New York State wine aficionados. With a minimalist approach to winemaking that today some would call "raw" or "natural" winemaking, Kim stopped using cultured yeasts in 2010 and does all fermentation with ambient or "wild" yeast. He uses no herbicides or insecti-

cides in the vineyards, and somewhat unusually his white wines see some extended skin contact.

The tasting room, located in Hector and open only on weekends or by appointment, is reminiscent of an old country cottage, and you can often find Kim and Debra pouring and chatting with visitors.

HECTOR WINE COMPANY

5610 NY State Route 414, Hector
607.387.1045
www.hectorwinecompany.com

Hector Wine Company is one of those perfect wine-country partnerships. Its co-owners are the friends, Jason Hazlitt, a viticulturist, and Justin Boyette, a winemaker. Grape growing is Jason's family business, and grapes for these wines come from Sawmill Creek Vineyards. The Hazlitt family has owned these vineyards and worked this land for seven generations. They can tell you stories about how the lake froze back in '74, and, when they say they know a little something about growing grapes in the Finger Lakes region, you can bet that that's an understatement.

Hector Wine Company opened its doors in 2010 and has created a reputation for producing quality wines in the short time since then. With less than 4,000 cases produced, the focus here is on quality and handcrafted vintages. As Jason and Justin will tell you, the vineyards overlook the deepest part of the lake, which retains enough heat for it almost never to freeze, protecting the vines in the harsh New York winters. This is one of the reasons why this vineyard is able to ripen a red-wine varietal you might not have sampled before: the Austrian grape

Blaufränkisch. Venues from *Forbes* magazine to the *New York Times* have lauded this unknown varietal in recent years, with *Forbes* declaring it the "best red you've never heard of," and Hector Wine Company is preparing for its first release any day now. Most wines range from $10 to $25.

LEIDENFROST VINEYARDS

5677 NY State Route 414, Hector
607.546.2800
www.leidenfrostwine.com

Leidenfrost is owned by one of the most established grape-growing families in the Finger Lakes area. The Leidenfrost family has been raising grapes since 1947, and they have here some of the earliest *vinifera* plantings in the Seneca Lake region, dating back to the 1980s, when the present owner, John Leidenfrost Jr., took over the winery.

Today, the winemaking and the wines at Leidenfrost have evolved right along with this increasingly celebrated region, but the tasting room still retains all of its original family-owned charms, and the annual case production is still limited to 3,000. John's daughter Elizabeth now helps him in the cellar, and together they make a range of whites, reds, and sparkling wines, mostly from *vinifera* varietals. There is also a good selection of cool-climate hybrid wines on offer, including the robust and full-bodied Baco Noir varietal that flourishes in the Finger Lakes, and the family is introducing some new varietals and techniques to the area. There are recent Gamay Noir plantings and a Hungarian barrel program that is worth keeping an eye on.

The winery boasts spectacular views of Seneca Lake, and they host a range of special events in springtime and summer, which are advertised on their website. Most wines are priced from $10 to $25.

SHALESTONE VINEYARDS

9681 NY State Route 414, Lodi
607.582.6600
www.shalestonevineyards.com

The folks at Shalestone believe in doing one thing and doing it well. "Red is all we do" is the motto here, and it's an audacious motto in a wine region with a relatively short growing season and one traditionally known for its whites. Shalestone in the only winery in the region focusing exclusively on red-wine varietals, though more and more of these varietals are being planted across the Finger Lakes AVA.

This is another family operation, run by the husband-and-wife

team of Rob and Kate Thomas, who are involved in every step of the process, from bud to bottle. Their son, Seth, joined them as vineyard manager and assistant winemaker in 2008. Rob has over three decades of winemaking experience in the area and is a consultant for several Finger Lakes wineries.

He aims for consistency in his wines across vintages, and production is under 1,500 cases.

The windows in their tasting room provide an almost cinematically perfect view of Seneca Lake, and when you're not busy taking in the scenery you can enjoy the cheeky and irreverent tasting notes that Rob and Kate provide to accompany the tastings. The technical sheet describes the 2011 Synergy (a Cabernet Sauvignon and Syrah blend), for example, as "A hard-working man of good muscle tone meets a cosmopolitan, long legged woman." Most wines are in the $15 to $35 range.

SILVER THREAD VINEYARD

1401 Caywood Road, Lodi
607.582.6116
www.silverthreadwine.com

Silver Thread's tasting room is on the eastern bank, between the Route 414 wine trail and Seneca Lake, and this charming winery has a distinctive "off-the-beaten-path" ambiance that makes it a favorite. The cozy tasting room, built in the style of a Swiss chalet, offers stunning views of the lake, and you will often find Paul and Shannon Brock, the husband-and-wife team who own and run Silver Thread, pouring the samples. In fact, when things get busy, Shannon's dad lends a helping hand, and this is very much a family-run business.

Paul and Shannon acquired Silver Thread in 2011 and, in the short time since, have established a reputation for producing one of the finest Rieslings in the region. Paul was previously a winemaker at Lamoreaux Landing, and Shannon worked at the New York State wine and culinary center. This is an excellent place to start if you want to understand why Finger Lakes Rieslings are internationally celebrated. Three of Silver Thread's Rieslings have scored 90 points in *Wine Spectator*, and, while the points and the recognition are nice, when tasting the wines

you'll quickly come to your own conclusions about what makes these wines special.

Paul and Shannon offer flight-style samplings of their single-vineyard Rieslings, which is a great way to learn more first-hand about the elusive concept of "terroir" and how wines from different vineyards and vineyard blocks can be so distinctive. They also offer a tasting experience with wine-and-chocolate pairings, with chocolates crafted by Hedonist Artisan Chocolates from Rochester. Silver Thread holds several annual special events, including a light-hearted Summer Solstice celebration, and details can be found on their website. Most wines are under the $20 price point.

If you find yourself at Silver Thread around lunchtime, drive up to Dano's Heuriger (pronounced Hoy-rig-er) on Seneca Lake, a one-of-a-kind Viennese-style lakeside restaurant where, weather permitting, you can sit outside and sample their delectable spreads or dig into a good old-fashioned Wiener Schnitzel.

KING'S GARDEN VINEYARDS

9085 NY State Route 414, Lodi, NY 14860
607.582.7444
www.kingsgardenvineyards.com

The cozy tasting room at King's Garden can get busy, but that doesn't stop the proprietor and winemaker here, Mike Oleksyn, from getting a chance to talk to everyone. Mike is generally the guy behind the tasting bar, and he's also the guy who makes these old-world-style red wines out in the cellars. The King's Garden offerings are rich and hearty wines that pair perfectly with substantial dishes. Mike's Syrah, with its distinct peppery notes, makes a delicious pairing with a rack of lamb or *steak au poivre*, and, if you want to experience firsthand the much-talked-about "vintage variation" in this wine-growing region,

try their Cabernet Sauvignon releases from different vintages side-by-side. You'll be surprised at the differences.

Red-wine varietals typically ripen later than white-wine varietals, and once again the key to Mike's success all starts with vineyard location. The 28-acre vineyard here, planted in 1998, is another planting in the "banana belt" sweet spot that's changing the reputation of Seneca Lake's wine production. Despite the large vineyard plantings and room to grow, Mike keeps things artisanal at King's Garden. The production is just under 3,000 cases. Most wines are in the $10 to $25 range.

BILLSBORO WINERY

4760 West Lake Road, Geneva
315.789.9538
www.billsborowinery.com

Perched on a small knoll overlooking Seneca Lake, the tasting room at Billsboro is conveniently located just five miles south of Geneva. Vinny and Kimberly Aliperti, the husband-and-wife team who are the proprietors here, release about ten wines each year, and this is a great first stop if you are looking for an introduction to this AVA and its varietals. Vinny honed his winemaking skills under the tutelage of the acclaimed winemaker Roman Roth at Wolffer Estate, and the couple has been in the Finger Lake's region since 2000. After working at the legendary Herman J. Weimar Vineyard for a year, Vinny joined Atwater Estate Vineyards, where he still works today as the head winemaker. Billsboro is the family's private project, and Kimberly manages its day-to-day operations.

Originally a barn from the 1870s, their tasting room is a great place to linger on a long, lazy afternoon. Pizza from their oven

Wine&Spirits
TRY A SAMPLE!!!
Chef Lerman
GRAPE SEED
OIL
WINE ENTHUSIAST
edible

on the patio and a bottle of Billsboro Riesling might be the wine country lunch you're looking for when it's warm enough to sit outside. They also regularly host live music events, vertical tastings, and library-wine tastings, if you're interested in entertainment or wine-education events. Check their website for details. Wines range from about $15 to $35, and case production is under 3000.

FOX RUN VINEYARDS

670 NY State Route 14, Penn Yan
800.636.9786
www.foxrunvineyards.com

In the eighties, Scott Osborn had a business in California selling ranches. Or, as he likes to say, *not selling* ranches. These were the days of interest rates in the teens, and business wasn't exactly booming. To keep himself busy, Scott got a job hand-labeling bottles in a winery in California. And—it's the classic wine-country story—he fell in love with wine in the process.

In 1985, when he came to visit family here in the Finger Lakes, he had an "epiphany," which arrived in the form a 1982 bottle of Wagner Chardonnay. This was probably the first cold-climate wine Scott had ever tasted, and he knew immediately that he wanted to make wines here. The rest, as they say, is history. When he announced his decision to winemaker friends in California, they warned him that it was so cold up here that wine would freeze in the barrel. He told them with his characteristic dry wit, well, that's less money spent on cold stabilization.

In 1992, Scott bought Fox Run Vineyards from the previous owners, who were selling because, as they said of the wine business, "It's not retirement." But Scott and his business partner, Andy, saw the potential, and they weren't looking for retirement anyhow.

Today, the winemaker at Fox Run Vineyards is Peter Bele, who honed his skills at, among other places, the legendary Dr. Konstantin Frank Vinifera Wine Cellars. Peter came to Fox Run with an international reputation, and his wines are poured in Michelin starred restaurants as far away as Antwerp, Belgium. Thanks to his formidable skills as a winemaker, the 90+ ratings from the wine pundits have already started pouring in for the Fox Run releases.

But this remains a low-key and friendly place, where you'll find a warm welcome if you're also just falling in love with New York State wines yourself. You can often find Scott in the tasting room, chatting with wine enthusiasts about his wines. If you do visit, be sure to ask for his talk on the Finger Lakes' geology. It's a super introduction to the unique *terroir* of the region. Wines from $10 to $45; case production is around 15,000.

RED TAIL RIDGE WINERY

846 NY State Route 14, Penn Yan
315.536.4580
www.redtailridgewinery.com

Mike Schnelle and Nancy Irelan, the husband-and-wife team at Red Tail Ridge, bought this thirty-five-acre parcel of land overlooking Seneca Lake in 2004. Mike had come from a career in heavy equipment and construction and brought with him a hands-on approach, which he first applied to clearing and planting the vineyard. The project, he will tell you, took him the better part of three years. Nancy came with a doctorate in grape genetics and more than a decade of experience at one of the world's largest wine producers, out in California.

Mike discovered they weren't the first people to clear this land during those three years of clearing and cutting. Buried in the fields, Mike and Nancy found nineteenth-century farming artifacts dating to the days when much of the northeast of the United States was an agrarian tapestry rather than pine forest. And, because Mike and Nancy were starting from scratch on the land and wanted to do it just so, they drew on Nancy's knowledge of the soils and climate and installed tile drainage throughout these relatively fertile soils to ensure that the vines suffer just enough. The result of this unfaltering attention to

detail is the excellent quality fruit that they use for their estate wine production.

If you're interested in how the winery world is changing and quickly moving toward sustainability measures, Mike and Nancy are on the forefront in New York State. Their facility was the first LEED-certified winery in the region. The heating and cooling is powered by geothermal systems, and everything from waste management to business practices are grounded in sustainability principles. Their commitment is reflected in their tasting room and wine sales too. Their "Good Karma" Riesling is a special community release, and they donate 10% of the proceeds to regional food banks.

The focus of the winemaking program at Red Tail Ridge tends toward the unusual and innovative. Mike and Nancy specialize in growing *vinifera*

varietals that you may not have encountered before. Fancy trying a Dornfelder or Toreldego wine? Dornfelder is a dark-skinned red-wine varietal developed in Germany in the 1950s. Toreldego is an ancient Italian varietal and related to Syrah, with characteristic notes that are bold and spicy. Wines range from $12 to $40, and there are often unique small barrel lots that sell out quickly.

KEMMETER WINES

1030 Larzelere Road, Penn Yan
315.521.3897
www.kemmeterwines.com

The winemaker and proprietor at Kemmeter Wines is Johannes Reinhardt. Johannes was born into a family of farmers and winemakers in a little village in Germany. Kemmeter is an old family name on his grandmother's side and a nod to those German roots and to tradition. After years of studying and working in wineries, large and small, in Germany, Johannes came to the United States in 1999 to work for a season at Dr. Konstantin Frank Vinifera Wine Cellars, the winery that helped to establish winemaking in the Finger Lakes. It turned out that Johannes never left. The next year, he accepted a position at Anthony Road Wine Company as the winemaker, where, for thirteen years, he produced some of the wines that established the reputation of the New York State wine country.

Today, though, Johannes has his own vineyard, planted in 2013 and located just across the street from Anthony Road. While his vineyard plantings of Riesling, Pinot Blanc and Pinot Noir mature, he is sourcing fruit from select growers in the region and is currently making a handful of wines. Johannes believes in taking time not just to hand craft his wines but also to enjoy them, which is why you will need to make an appointment with Johannes if you want to do a tasting. If you come, be sure to leave plenty of time. Unhurried is the name of the game here. Most wines are in the $15 to $30 range.

ANTHONY ROAD WINE COMPANY

1020 Anthony Road, Penn Yan
315.536.2182
www.anthonyroadwine.com

The Martini family has worked this land for over forty years. John and Ann Martini moved to the region in 1973 and planted eighty acres of vineyards overlooking Seneca Lake, long before winemaking in New York State seemed all that sensible. They initially sold grapes to producers across the state and, after about fifteen years, decided to open their own winery. Anthony Road has grown since then but remains, at heart, a family-run operation, and their forward-looking vision now looks prescient. John and Ann's four children all grew up in the business, and son Peter Martini is the vineyard manager. For the

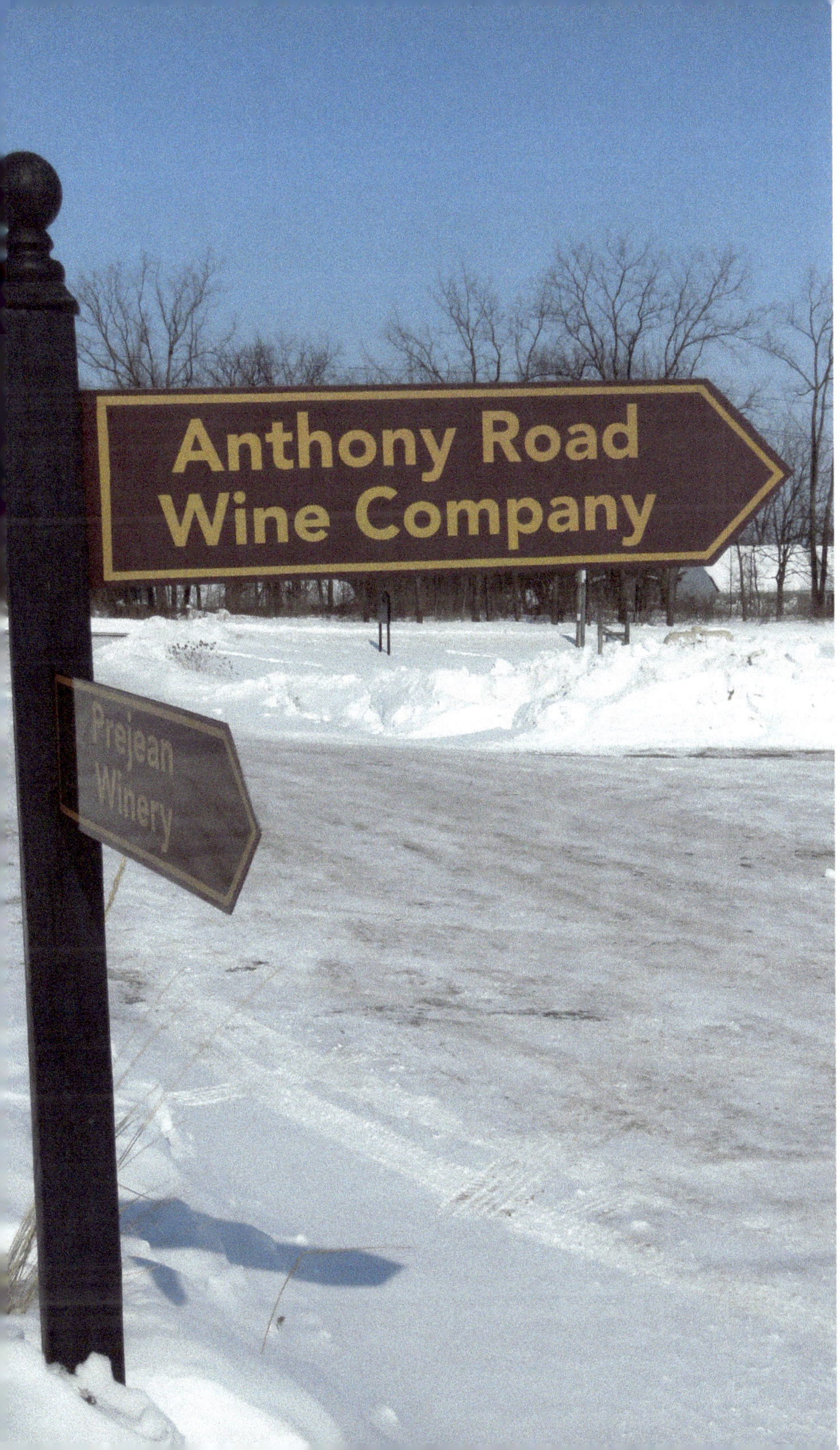
Anthony Road
Wine Company
Prejean
Winery

last twenty years, John has made the trip to the Union Square farmer's market in New York City almost every week to share his wines and his passion, so if you live in Manhattan and can't make it upstate, you can sample the Anthony Road wines in the City.

But it would be a shame to miss the chance to see the Anthony Road winery or the chance to take in the beauties of the Finger Lakes if you have the opportunity. The tasting room is located just off of Route 14, about ten miles south of Geneva, on the west side of the lake. The bright and light-filled tasting room also doubles as an art gallery, displaying work from local artists, with exhibits changing on a monthly basis. In the warmer

months, picnic tables outside the tasting room are a perfect place to while away an afternoon with a picnic lunch and a bottle of your newest tasting-room favorite. If you can't decide, we recommend checking out their Cabernet Franc Rosé. It's the perfect picnic wine and was voted the best Rosé in New York State in a recent vintage.

Most wines range from about $10 to $45, and reservations are recommended for large groups.

HERMANN J. WIEMER VINEYARD

3962 NY State Route 14, Dundee, NY 14837
607.243.7971
www.wiemer.com

Hermann J. Wiemer arrived in the Finger Lakes from Germany in the 1960s. This was a time when there was very little *vinifera* cultivated here, and Hermann came from a long tradition of winemaking. His mother's family had been making wine for over three hundred years in Mosel, Germany. His father was responsible for restoring vines in Mosel after the destruction caused by the Second World War. When Hermann arrived in the Finger Lakes, he found that the climate and soil here was similar to that in Mosel, so he bought eighty acres of land on the western shore of Seneca Lake and spent countless hours grafting Riesling vines to American rootstock, looking for the best varietal suited to the region. His innovations altered the course of this wine region's history.

Today, the winery that Hermann founded is one of New York State's premium "legacy" wineries, where history and great winemaking come together. And while some estate vineyards are passed from parents to children, the Hermann J. Wiemer winery has descended from teacher to pupils. Fred Merwarth, Hermann's long-term apprentice, and Oskar Bynke, a Swedish agronomist and Merwath's friend from Cornell University, took over the winery in 2003. Today, Fred and Oskar make wines that combine winemaking know-how perfected over centuries with innovative research to continue Hermann's search for the best varietals and vineyard techniques.

It is no surprise that their wines routinely garner international acclaim or that this is one of the most talked-about wineries in the area. *The New York Times* notes that

77

"Wiemer is considered one of the top Riesling producers in the United States," and their semi-dry Riesling was poured at one of President Obama's dinners at the Red Rooster restaurant in New York City.

The tasting room at Hermann J. Wiemer is an experience in itself, however. It was recently gut-renovated with materials sourced locally and with wood reclaimed from a nearby barn dating to the 1800s. Instead of one big tasting room, Fred and Oskar opted for a design that makes for a more intimate and private tasting experience, and the winery also offers special tastings in the cellars, where you can witness firsthand the winemaking process.

Most wines here are in the $15 to $40 range, with the exception of the "Noble Rot" wines, which are priced higher and for good reason. You will not want to leave without tasting these late-harvest dessert wines, which are produced in years when the grapes experience a bloom of the "noble" fungus *Botrytis cinerea*, which dries the fruit naturally on the vines and concentrates the sugars and the aromas. The Wiemer estate produces these wines in the classic German and Austrian styles, and during your travels in the New York State wine country, you may see terms like *Beerenauslese* (sweet) and *Trockenbeerenau-*

slese (sweeter) for ice wines and late-harvest productions. If you're keen to learn more, this is the place to ask the winemaker.

BARNSTORMER WINERY

4184 NY State Route 14, Rock Stream
607.243.4008
www.barnstormerwinery.com

Back in the Roaring Twenties, Barnstormers were pilots who flew throughout the country selling airplane rides and performing stunts. Named after these high-flying early stuntmen, the Barnstormer winery describes itself as a "fine blend of tradition and adventure." And, who knows, maybe folks once watched those by-gone Barnstormers from the winery site. The winery is a 150-year-old barn that's been converted into a charming tasting room and production facility.

You can often find owner Scott Bronstein pouring in the tasting room, and this is very much a small, artisanal project for Scott, who sources his fruit from grape growers in the Seneca and Cayuga Lake regions. Some of the Barnstormer wines are also getting attention on the national stage. Scott's 2013 dry Riesling got 86 points with the *Wine Spectator,* and, if you're looking for something interesting and unusual, the Sangiovese Rosé is a standout. Scott also pours craft beer from the tasting room, and, should you start to feel peckish on the tasting trail, you can pick up cheese and charcuterie picnic supplies here that

you can enjoy on-site or can take with you. There is a summer concert series and other special events, advertised on the website. Most wines are priced under $20, except for the ice wine and the reserve Cabernet Sauvignon, which are priced modestly higher.

Keuka Lake

● Winery

Italy Hill Rd.

Hunt Country
Vineyards

54A

Rooster Hill
Vineyards

14A

54

54A

Keuka Lake

McGregor
Vineyards

230

1

Ravines Wine
Cellars

Dr. Konstantin
Frank Wine Cellars

Domaine
Leseurre Winery

226

Keuka Lake
Vineyards

54

Keuka Lake

SOUTHWEST OF SENECA LAKE IS KEUKA LAKE, AND, WHILE SENE-ca Lake's tasting trail is comparatively busy and well-travelled, Keuka is quieter and still largely undiscovered. What this means in practice is that many of the wineries around Keuka Lake are still only open on the weekends. Even on weekends, it's generally best to call ahead to see if a winery is open or to make a reservation. However, don't let this put you off. This wine region won't be undeveloped or undiscovered for long, and here's your chance to be one of the first of the aficionados. The scenery here is spectacular and you can still make discoveries on the back lanes. You'll find quiet country roads that open up onto long vistas over steep hills and sloping lakeside vineyards, and you'll be amply rewarded for that bit of extra effort.

DOMAINE LESEURRE WINERY

13920 NY State Highway 54, Hammondsport
607.292.3920
www.domaineleseurre.com

You have likely never heard of the husband-and-wife winemaking team of Sébastien and Céline LeSuerre. But it's likely that you will, sooner or later. Sébastien and Céline are both from France, but that's not where their romance started. They met while working in a vineyard in New Zealand. Naturally, it was those shared roots and a shared love for wines that led them both to the vineyard. Sébastien hails from a winemaking family in the Champagne area, with over six generations of winemaking experience. Céline comes from the Toulouse area of southwestern of France and grew up in a vineyard in the foothills of the Pyrenees.

After working in vineyards in different countries as a young couple, Sébastien and Céline visited the Finger Lakes, fell in love with the Keuka Lake region, and decided to establish their family winery here. Their first vintage was bottled in 2012, and

they opened the doors of their tasting room in late 2013. They currently make just a few hundred cases of some exquisite white wines, including an exceptional Chardonnay, and just one red wine, a Pinot Noir. They source the fruit from various carefully selected growers in the region, and Céline will tell you how, for their first vintage, Sébastien tasted grapes at over four hundred vineyards before they settled on their contracts. They have recently purchased the land for their future estate vineyards and are preparing the soil for plantings.

The tasting room is located on State Route 54 in Hammondsport, on the western shore of Keuka Lake. The French-accented tasting room has views of the lake and is a cozy spot for an extended tasting. Most wines range from $15 to $25 and are a good bargain.

RAVINES WINE CELLARS

14630 State Route 54, Hammondsport
607.292.7007
www.ravineswine.com

Ravines Wine Cellars is the happy marriage of winemaker and oenologist Morten Hallgren and chef Lisa Hallgren. Morten grew up on a wine estate in Provence, in southern France, and studied oenology and viticulture in the prestigious program at Montpellier, eventually becoming the chief winemaker at the landmark Dr. Konstantin Frank's wine cellars in Keuka Lake. Lisa is a food arti-

san who creates recipes featuring local and seasonal ingredients that pair beautifully with their food-friendly wines.

While their vineyard is perched between two eponymous ravines on the shores of Keuka Lake, the tasting room on State Route 54 is their estate outpost. Here, on the eastern shore of Keuka Lake, the tasting room is styled as a French bistro, and they feature chocolate-and-wine pairings, with chocolate sourced from local craft suppliers. Ravines Wine Cellars makes a nice selection of dry white wines, red wines, and sparkling wines, as well as a few dessert wines. Prices range from $12 - $40, with most wines under $25. The tasting room is open daily during the spring and summer, and there are more limited winter hours, posted on their website.

McGREGOR VINEYARD

5503 Dutch Street, Dundee
607.292.3999
www.mcgregorwinery.com

The family who runs McGregor Vineyards was another of the early growers to plant *vinifera* vines in the Finger Lakes, which they did back in the early 1970s, when growers and winemakers in the region still widely believed that these European grapes could not survive the harsh winters. The McGregors were betting that this was wrong. And it was a sizable gamble. They planted not one but nearly twenty-eight acres on the shores of Keuka Lake, where the land slopes much more steeply than in the other large lakes in the region.

Today, McGregor Vineyard makes a variety of reds and whites, including wines made from some grape varietals that are comparatively rare in North America. These include grape varietals such as Rkatsiteli, Sereksiya Charni, and Saperavi, from Georgia and Moldova in Eastern Europe and the areas around the Black and Caspian seas. These are robust, aromatic wines and have caught the

attention of trade magazines such as the *Wine Enthusiast,* not for their rarity but for their quality. McGregor's signature blend, the Sereksiya Charni-and-Saperavi duo that they have dubbed "Black Russian Red," has especially acquired a cult following since it was first introduced. Saperavi means "paint" or "dye" in Georgian, an apt name given the intense dark red color of the wine made with this varietal. Until recently, this was the only winery in the United States using Saperavi to make a commercially sold wine, and today only a handful of vine-yards grow this grape in North America.

As their name suggests, however, the McGregor family does not hail from Georgia. Their Scottish ancestry is reflected in the tasting room and their summer live music choices. The tasting room features an enclosed deck overlooking Keuka Lake, and, in the summer, you can enjoy live entertainment on Saturday evenings while sipping wine and sampling local cheeses on the outdoor picnic tables. Annual case production is just under 8,000 cases, and most wines range from $15 to $40.

ROOSTER HILL VINEYARDS

489 NY State Route 54, Penn Yan
315.536.4773
www.roosterhill.com

There is a saying in the wine industry that there are two ways to get started in the business: either you have a long family history in the vineyard or you had a successful first career. In the case of Amy and David Hoffman, the proprietors at Rooster Hill Vineyards, they came to make wine via the second route, after they left corporate jobs in Southern California. They moved to Keuka Lake in 2000 to pursue their wine-country dream, buying eight acres of a neglected plot of land overlooking the lake. Within a few years, they had transformed it into a vineyard.

Today, they make a range of red and white wines, as well as a port wine, and they use both estate fruit and selected fruit from other growers in the area. Less than a decade into their dream, they have already been featured in *Wine Spectator* and *Wine Enthusiast.* The tasting room is Tuscan-style, with brightly painted walls, and the ambiance is very much *la dolce vita.* During the warmer months, the porch overlooking the lake is open, and you're welcome to linger if you need to regroup after all that grueling wine tasting. Wines range from $12 to $25, and production is just under 5,000 cases.

HUNT COUNTRY VINEYARDS

4021 Italy Hill Road, Branchport
315.595.2812
www.huntwines.com

Art and Joyce Hunt, the husband-wife team behind Hunt Country Vineyards, are high-school sweethearts who hail from Corning, New York. In 1973, after pursuing careers in insurance sales and social work, respectively, the couple moved to the 170-acre farm belonging to Art's grandfather. They then planted fifty acres of vineyard with no intention except selling the fruit to other producers.

As is the way in wine country, things changed. In 1987, Hunt Country Vineyards was born, and Art and Joyce started making their own wines. Today, their son, Jonathan, directs the winemaking program, and he is the sixth generation Hunt to help run this family farmland. Perhaps it is this long connection with the land that makes sustainability such a priority for the Hunts. As they will tell you, they have undertaken a host of green initiatives in the past few years and have been able to reduce their carbon footprint by almost 50% since 2007. All the food and wine products sold in their tasting room are sourced locally.

Their wines have won numerous awards and accolades, including medals in several national-level competitions for their ice wine and their late harvest Moscato. They make a range of wines from *vinifera*, French-American hybrids, and *labrusca* grapes. Most wines are priced in the $10 to $20 range.

DR. KONSTANTIN FRANK VINIFERA WINE CELLARS

9749 Middle Road, Hammondsport
800.320.0735
www.drfrankwines.com

In 1951, a man arrived in New York City from what is now called Ukraine and found a job as a dishwasher. He spoke nine languages. English, however, was not one of them.

He had a doctorate in viticulture and had written his thesis on growing *Vitis vinifera* in cold climates. While for the moment,

he was a dishwasher, in the years to come, he would almost single-handedly change the course of wine history in New York State and in the cool-climate wine regions of North America.

Before Dr. Konstantin Frank's arrival in New York State, most of the grapes grown in the Finger Lakes area were *Vitis labrusca*, a native grape species. Ridiculed for the notion that *vinifera* could survive in New York State's cold climate, Dr. Frank set out to prove that it could. The plants would, admittedly, need some assistance. So, Dr. Frank grafted *vinifera* vines to *labrusca* rootstocks and changed forever this wine region.

Almost half a century later, the plot of land where he planted these early vines is home to the winery he also founded, and it is one of the country's most highly celebrated producers. When

you head to the tasting room overlooking Keuka Lake, the first thing to greet you are the rows-upon-rows of wine bottles, laden with medals from wine competitions, local and international. Dr. Frank's son, Willy Frank, also became a winemaker with a passion for sparkling wine and founded Chateau Frank, located just down the road from the main tasting room. Dr. Frank's grandson now manages the family estate's productions.

Unlike the other "back-lane" wineries in the area, this is not a small production. It would be hard to call the Dr. Frank winery

a boutique, though it is family-owned and the roads leading to it are quaintly winding. However, the popularity of the wines, the accolades, and the landmark history have all ensured that production here is now mid-sized and flourishing. But as a landmark, and as an exceptional New York State producer, leave time on your tasting adventures for a visit. After all, this is where it all started.

KEUKA LAKE VINEYARDS

8882 County Road 76, Hammondsport
607.868.4100
www.klvineyards.com

Keuka Lake Vineyards is a small farmstead winery, and it is as unpretentious as it is charming. So, you might be surprised to learn that it was named on a list of the hundred best wineries in the United States in 2014, and their wines have repeatedly garnered points in the 90s from *Wine Spectator.* Their wines are poured at more than forty of New York City's top restaurants, including Bar Boulud, Gramercy Tavern, and the Spotted Pig. So, if you're curious, and can't get up to the wine country, you can start your research in the city.

But this is one of those places where you're welcome to do more than just come up for a tasting. Each year, they invite visitors and wine enthusiasts to come pitch in for the Riesling harvest (see their website for details). It is a remarkable and gratifyingly exhausting experience. But if a harvest intern holiday weekend isn't in the cards, certainly stop by for the tasting. The wines on offer here are largely *vinifera*, alongside some select hybrid varieties, and some of the warmest accolades have been reserved for those hybrids. If you want to see what is possible with these varietals—especially with Leon Millot—these

are some of the folks bearing the standard. The tasting room is on the southwest side of Keuka Lake, on County Road 76 in Hammondsport, and offers chocolate and wine pairings, with artisanal chocolates sourced locally. Most wines range from $15 to $35, with a total case production of around 3,000.

Cayuga Lake

● Winery

89

Heart &
Hands Wine
Company

90

34B

34

Cayuga
Lake

Hosmer
Winery

Sheldrake Point
Winery

90

89

34B

34

Americana Vineyards
& Winery

96

34B

79

13

20

20

20

ALMOST FORTY MILES IN LENGTH, CAYUGA LAKE IS THE LONGEST and easternmost of the Finger Lakes. The town of Ithaca is located at the southern end of the lake and is home to Cornell University and Ithaca College. Because of this, it has a youthful and bohemian vibe and plenty of great restaurants. This lake is also very popular among recreational boaters and has a large marina on its southern end, in Ithaca.

The scenic area around the lake offers vistas of rolling farm-lands, vineyards, and striking waterfalls and gorges. (Local bumper stickers proclaim: "Ithaca is Gorges.") The Cayuga Lake AVA has more than two-dozen wineries, a handful of distill-eries, and a cidery. Established in 1983, the Cayuga Wine Trail is America's first organized, and longest-running, wine trail. Due to its lower altitude, the growing season for Cayuga Lake is somewhere between 190 and 205 days, making it the longest in the Finger Lakes. That means this area can also ripen fruit just that bit more reliably than some other AVAs in the New York State region.

If you're pressed on time, start on the western shore, at either end, as most of the wineries are located in the northern and southern third of the western shore of the lake. If you're lucky enough to have ample time, carry on along the eastern shore as well, and you will be rewarded with plenty of scenic stops, as well new tasting discoveries.

HEART & HANDS WINE COMPANY

4162 New York State Route 90, Union Springs
315.889.8500
www.heartandhandswine.com

Tom Higgins grew up in the Finger Lakes wine country and, after completing his education, decided to enter the technology industry to ride the dot-com boom of the 1990s. It was during this time that he met his wife Susan, who shared his passion for wine. For Tom, the tech industry was interesting enough, and he longed to return to the wine country. But the Finger Lakes wasn't the first stop in what turned out to be a somewhat roundabout journey home. Tom first worked in Bordeaux, at Château La Lagune, where he learned old-world winemaking techniques in the cellars. He moved on to work in California, as a harvest intern at Calera Wine Company, one of the pioneer producers of Pinot Noir in California.

But when Tom and Susan founded their own winery at last, he headed home to the Finger Lakes. Tom founded Hearts & Hands in 2006, after finding a vineyard and tasting-room site

on the eastern shores of Cayuga Lake that was ideally suited to Pinot Noir and Riesling.

Today, estate Pinot Noir and Riesling wines remain the only two wines Heart & Hands produce, but those two varietals are remarkably versatile, and Tom makes wines in several different styles from these two grapes, including a Rosé, a white Pinot Noir, and a limited-production late-harvest Riesling. Case

production is under 2,000, and the grapes are hand-harvested, with only the best clusters being retained.

In addition to traditional back-lane wine-tasting experiences, they also offer premier barrel tastings, so wine lovers can take a peek into their winemaking process. The tasting room is open on weekends and on weekdays by appointment. Most wines are in the $20 to $40 range.

HOSMER WINERY

7020 New York State Route 89, Ovid
607.869.3393
www.hosmerwinery.com

Cameron's father, a Syracuse textile manufacturer, dreamed of growing grapes at the family's summer home on the shore of Cayuga Lake, land that had been in the family since the 1920s. That dream took its first step towards reality when Cameron and his wife, Maren, first planted grapevines here in the 1970s, on just five acres of land. After a decade and a half of selling grapes to others, Cameron and Maren decided to make their own wine in the late 1980s. The family has never looked back. Hosmer Winery has now grown to seventy acres of thriving vineyards, tended by Cameron and his son, Timothy. Today, their Patrician Verona vineyard produces about 8,000 cases of wine.

Located on the western shore of Cayuga Lake, just twenty miles north of Ithaca on State Route 89, the vineyard also houses the tasting room and the production facility. Huge believers in allowing *terroir* to find expression in the bottle and practitioners of what they call "non-interventional winemaking," the Hosmer family has launched their signature "Single Wheel Riesling" as

their most concentrated exemplar. They describe this wine as "One season, one site, one variety" in a bottle.

The winemaker at Hosmer, Aaron Roisen, studied viticulture in New Zealand, and Aaron joined Hosmer as head winemaker in 2007. His wines have received warm reviews from the *Wine Enthusiast* and accolades in several New York State wine competitions. Hosmer Winery makes a range of offerings, including sparkling and dessert wines, and almost all their wines are reasonably priced in the $10 to $25 range.

SHELDRAKE POINT WINERY

7448 County Road 153, Ovid
607.532.9401
www.sheldrakepoint.com

The vineyards at Sheldrake Point are located on a patch of land so unique that the wines here could be a case study on the impact of *terroir* in winemaking. The vineyards are spread over forty-four acres that rest between two gorges, on a slope facing Cayuga Lake, with a difference in elevation of about 120 feet between the highest and lowest points. This gives the vineyard a ten to fifteen degree temperature difference, with delicate

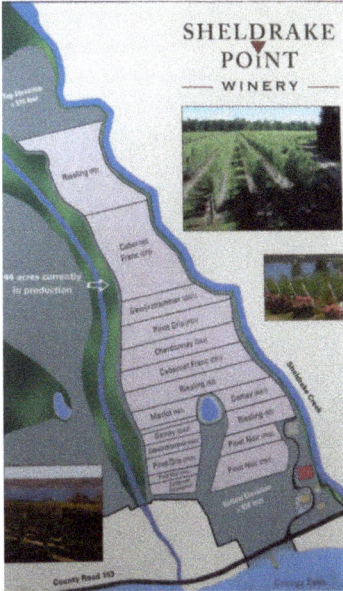

varieties planted toward the lower elevation, so as to benefit from the warming influence of the lake. The folks at Sheldrake lovingly call this the "Sheldrake effect," and they swear it is part of this vineyard's secret.

Of course, this patch of land wasn't always a vineyard. For much of its history, it was a dairy farm. The reason for

its transformation is the owner, Chuck Tauck, who converted the abandoned farm into the present-day winery and tasting room. Dave Breeden, the winemaker at Sheldrake Point, brings a combination of a meticulous scientific method and an artisan's touch to his winemaking style, and he experiments with wild ferments and native yeasts in Sheldrake ice wines ($100) to supplement the *terroir* expression. The Cabernet Franc Rosé, though, is their bestseller, and most wines are in the $15 to $30 range.

AMERICANA VINEYARDS & WINERY

4367 East Covert Road, Interlaken
607.387.6801
www.americanavineyards.com

Two chocolate Labs, Max and Rubie, are the welcoming "winery dog" committee here at Americana Vineyards. From the moment you step out of the car, they will lead you, eagerly, to the tasting room, a restored 1820s swing barn that was originally located five miles from its current location. It was meticulously dismantled and rebuilt at this new address. Today, the rustic interior is accented with farmhouse-style décor and there is a long luxurious porch wrapping the front and sides, perfect for slow summer afternoon wine tasting.

They make a range of wines at Americana, mostly from *vinifera* but also from some non-*vinifera* grapes as well, and many of their wines are nationally and internationally acclaimed. During the summer months, there is an impressive list of concerts and events by local musicians. The tasting room also sells homemade fudge, and there's a new taproom and beer garden, with a selection of local brews on tap. The tasting room is both kid and pet-friendly.

Several years ago, the winery opened a second venue on the same site as the tasting room, Crystal Lake Café, which is a great stop for lunch around Cayuga Lake, with an emphasis on locally sourced ingredients. If you're looking for a good brunch spot on the tasting trail, the Crystal Lake Café is a local favorite. That means, of course, that the tables on Sunday fill up quickly, so arrive as close to opening time as possible if you want a guaranteed spot at the table.

Eating

EVERYONE WORKS UP AN APPETITE AFTER A LONG MORNING OR evening wine tasting. After all, lugging all your finds to the trunk of your car for the long-haul home to your cellar is a hard business. Fortunately, there are dozens of excellent small cafés and bistros throughout the Finger Lakes, many featuring local foods and wines, and new venues are opening (and, alas, closing) daily. Here are some of the best picks we've discovered.

FLX WIENERY

5090 New York State Route 14, Dundee
607.243.7100
www.flxwinery.com

If you're tooling about on the west side of Seneca Lake or if you're willing to drive to get your fix of authentic German street food, FLX Wienery is a top pick for lunch in the area. The currywurst might just be the best this side of Berlin, and there is a beer selection worthy of Oktoberfest. There are also artisanal hot dogs and hamburgers on offer. For the health conscious, there are buckwheat and quinoa salads as well. The quirky interior is Route 66 Americana, with a hipster food truck twist.

Isabel Bogadtke and her husband, business partner, and master sommelier, Christopher Bates, own and run FLX Wienery, and they have worked in the hospitality industry in Berlin, Italy, and Texas, among other places.

FLX Wienery

GENEVA ON THE LAKE

1001 Lochland Road, Geneva
315.789.7190
www.genevaonthelake.com

If you're planning a romantic weekend get-away with that some-one special or looking for a date-night dinner in the New York State wine country, the Lan-cellotti dining room at the palatial Italianate villa Geneva on the Lake is the answer. The resort is also open for overnight accommodation and weekend packages. Pampering here means candlelit dinners with live piano music overlooking lush lawns sloping down into Seneca Lake. This historic resort epitomizes old-world charm and was featured in the book *1000 Places to See Before You Die.* The restaurant offers an excellent selection of Finger Lakes wines and quality fare produced from local purveyors.

SUZANNE FINE REGIONAL CUISINE

9013 New York State Route 414, Lodi
607.582.7545
www.suzannefrc.com

Chef Suzanne's restaurant, set in a century-old farmhouse, is hands-down the best spot for fine dining this side of Seneca Lake. They offer over a hundred Finger Lakes wine selections and have been awarded the Wine Spectator Award of Excellence for their outstanding wine list. With the stiff competition among restaurants when it comes to wine lists, this is quite an achievement. Besides being a restaurant, they also run a cooking school, and host private dining and special events.

DANO'S HEURIGER

9564 New York State Route 414, Lodi
607.582.7555
www.danosonseneca.com

Dano's Heuriger (pronounced Hoy-rig-er) on the eastern shore
of Seneca Lake is a one-of-a-kind Viennese-style lakeside
restaurant where you can sample delectable spreads or dig into
a good old-fashioned Wiener schnitzel. In warmer months,
there is an outside patio as well for leisurely *al fresco* lunches
and dinners. Owned and operated by Dano Hutnik and pastry
chef Karen Gilman, Dano's is a local favorite.

Byways & Distractions

HECTOR FALLS

A celebrated roadside "beauty spot" and waterfall located on the southeast shore of Seneca Lake on Route 414, Hector Falls is your wine-country photo-op and a chance to take in some of the famous local scenery. Parking is on the shoulder of the road, and the views are most impressive in the spring and autumn, and after a heavy downpour.

BEER TASTING

The Finger Lakes is emerging as a go-to destination for craft beer lovers as well as wine lovers, with scores of microbreweries, brew pubs, and tap-houses opening in the area. Current estimates are that there are nearly a hundred craft breweries and brew pubs in the area, and that number is growing rapidly. One of the key factors that makes the region well-suited for beer brewing is the local access to exceptionally clean water. After all, beer is over 90 percent water. Also, brewers here will tell you that the fresh lake water contributes to the flavor of their brews. Locally grown hops and barley are used by many of the brewers in their creations. The region today hosts craft-beer festivals, expos, and beer tasting itineraries, and tours can be found year-round.

Some of the thanks for this renaissance in the brewing craft is New York State's Farm Brewery Law, which offers financial incentives to brewers for using local ingredients. Like any other industry coming of age, the brewers here are pushing the creative boundaries of taste and style, which makes it a great moment to hop on a beer trail in the area. The Finger Lakes Beer Trail (www.fingerlakesbeertrail.com), launched in 2011, is your best early guide to the region's breweries, brew pubs, and tap-houses.

THE
North
Fork

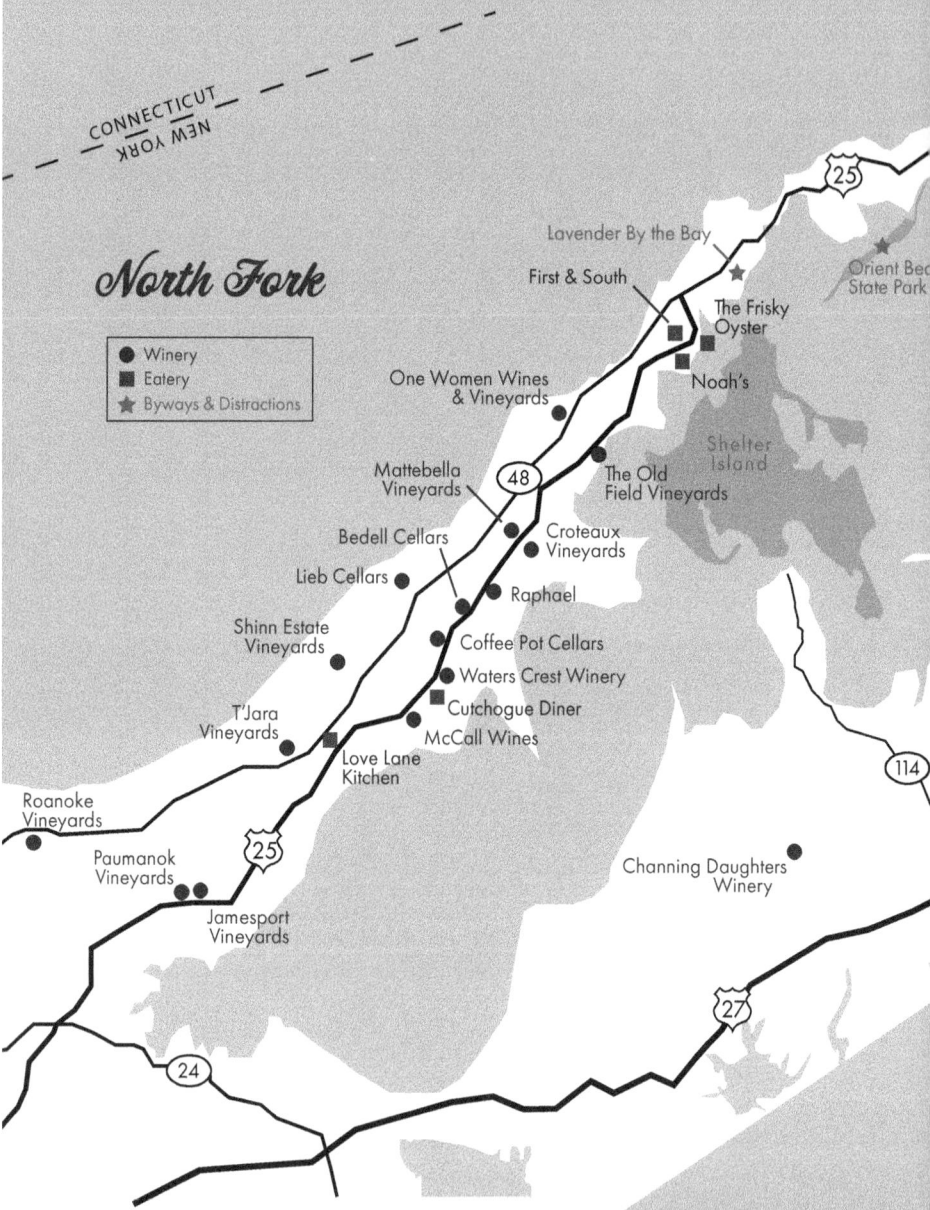

North Fork

Legend:
- ● Winery
- ■ Eatery
- ★ Byways & Distractions

CONNECTICUT
NEW YORK

Lavender By the Bay
First & South
The Frisky Oyster
Noah's
One Women Wines & Vineyards
Shelter Island
Orient Beach State Park
Mattebella Vineyards
The Old Field Vineyards
Bedell Cellars
Croteaux Vineyards
Lieb Cellars
Raphael
Shinn Estate Vineyards
Coffee Pot Cellars
Waters Crest Winery
T'Jara Vineyards
Cutchogue Diner
McCall Wines
Love Lane Kitchen
Roanoke Vineyards
Paumanok Vineyards
Jamesport Vineyards
Channing Daughters Winery

25
48
114
27
24

THE TWENTY-SEVEN MILE STRETCH OF LAND BETWEEN Riverhead and Orient is the North Fork of Long Island, an area that is currently witnessing a wine revolution. As the locals here will tell you, the North Fork is at the same latitude as Bordeaux, and some intrepid and pioneering souls are trying their hands at planting Merlot, Cabernet Sauvignon, and Cabernet Franc—traditional Bordeaux varietals. Others in the area are perfecting the cool-climate white wine varietals for which New York State was first celebrated, especially Gewürztraminers and Rieslings. But, increasingly, growers are also experimenting with crisp cool-climate Chardonnay wines and Sauvignon Blancs and Viogniers wines that clearly reflect the maritime climate of the area.

Say what you will about latitude, but, apart from a similar growing season and early success with Bordeaux varietals, the area is markedly different from its French cousin. For one thing, land here is scarce and vastly expensive due to its proximity to New York City. However, this can be a blessing in disguise: it creates the perfect conditions for extreme "boutique" and even *garagiste* winemaking. Few winemakers here have more than a small case production. Winemaking here is also not for the faint of heart. The winters are harsh and the weather can be foul and unpredictable on the Eastern Seaboard. Winemakers will readily tell you stories of how harvest decisions were made during the years of the major hurricanes to hit this area recently—stories of grit, passion, and luck that will make you appreciate all the more the wine you that are sampling.

To visit the North Fork at this point in time is to witness a wine region that is coming of age, and that is growing up quickly. Producers here are already making some wines that have achieved international acclaim and are conducting some bold experiments in winemaking. The first winery in this region, Hargrave, was only established in 1973. Today, there is a clearly established and quickly growing tasting trail. Technically, Long Island has two AVAs—the North Fork and the Hamptons. The North Fork has about forty wineries in operation today

and the Hamptons (on the "South Fork") a handful more. The area, however, has less than 3,000 acres in cultivation and only makes about 500,000 cases annually. Unlike the Finger Lakes area, the North Fork is almost exclusively devoted to growing *vinifera* grapes and grows over twenty classic varietals.

The entire length of the North Fork, from Riverhead in the east to the tip of the island at Orient, is forty minutes by car, but should take much longer if you are doing it right when you're out tasting. Most of the wineries are located on or between the two arterial roads that run the length of the North Fork: Middle Road in the north and Route 25 just south of it. Greenport has some of the area's best restaurants, where you can sample some more local wine while indulging in the area's exceptional seafood. If you're looking to stay overnight, there are many cozy

bed and breakfasts in the area, most of them family-run and most with an ambiance determined to transport you to another era and help you wind down after your wine travels. Arbor View House in East Marion, run by Wilfred and Veda Joseph, is one great choice. Veda's breakfast is famous among their repeat visitors and regulars. Other excellent options include the inviting Stirling House Bed and Breakfast in Greenport, the charming Harvest Inn in Peconic, and the Fig and Olive Bed and Breakfast in Cutchogue. A list of many other B&Bs in the area can also be found on the website of the North Fork Bed and Breakfast Association (www.nfbba.org).

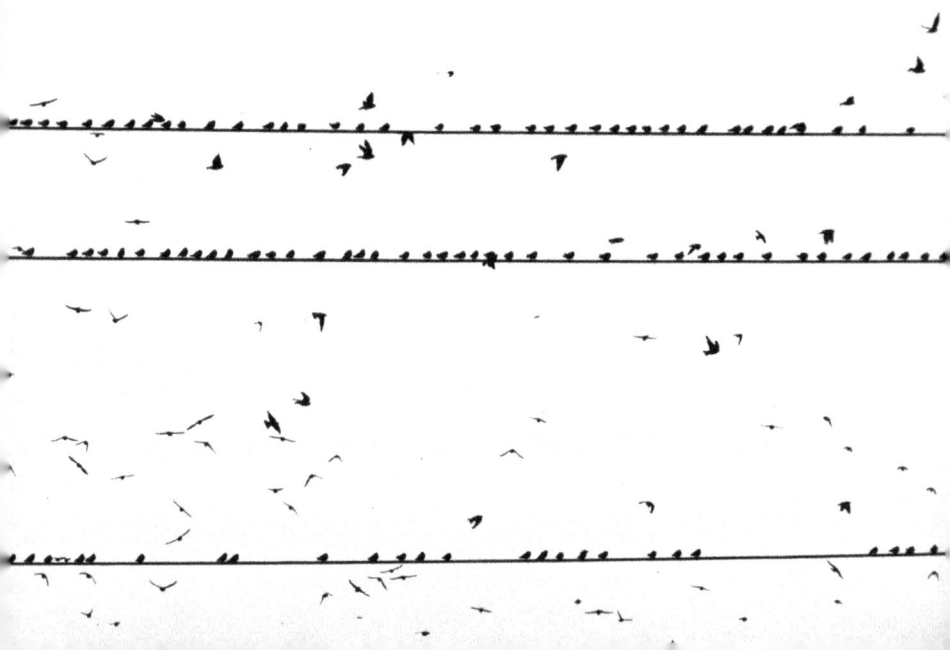

THE OLD FIELD

59600 Main Road, Southold
631.765.0004
www.theoldfield.com

When Chris Baiz and Ros Phelps took over the nineteenth-century tavern and farm at Old Field, they became the fourth generation in their family to work a stretch of about twelve acres that is one of the most picturesque and storied pieces of farmland in the North Fork. The Old Field is the second oldest winery in the North Fork, started at a time when doing so in this part of the country was still considered brave and perhaps just a bit foolish. But that independent spirit has paid off for the family. The vineyard overlooks beautiful Southold Bay, with views toward Shelter Island, and due to a unique microclimate, the vineyard often stays a full ten degrees cooler than other areas of the property.

The tasting at Old Field starts with the sparkling Blanc de Noir, generally considered one of the best from this AVA. The family also produces an excellent quality Merlot. The label on that wine is a black ship, and if you ask Ros will tell you the story behind the ship and their ancestor, "Commodore Perry," for whom the wine is named. She might also regale you with stories about the time Oscar-winning actresses Anna Paquin and Katie Holmes were onsite here during the filming of the movie "The Romantics."

Production is usually around 1,500 cases, with prices ranging from about $18 to $40.

MATTEBELLA VINEYARDS

46005 New York State Route 25, Southold
631.655.9554
www.mattebella.com

Owner and winemaker Mark Tobin's tasting room at Mattebella is truly a family affair. He and his wife, Christine Tobin,
named the winery after their children, Matthew and Isabella,
and on most days the young Tobin family can be found having
as much fun as the visitors, who on the day of our visit seemed
to have gone quickly from sampling to ordering bottles. Their

non-vintage "Famiglia Red," a Merlot and Cabernet-Franc blend, is an unpretentious wine that successfully does what it is meant to do, serving as a versatile table wine that pairs well with a wide range of foods. The fruit comes from their twenty-two-acre single vineyard, located just off of Route 25. The outdoor tasting area is also an inviting location to try their "Old World Red" blend to the soundtrack of some French music. Wines are in the $20 to $55 range.

CROTEAUX VINEYARDS

1450 South Harbor Road, Southold
631.765.6099
www.croteaux.com

"Rosé on Purpose" is the mission statement here. The husband-and-wife team of Michael and Paula Croteaux set out to do one thing when they opened their winery: to make the kind of Rosé wine that evokes lazy summer afternoons in Provence. In the process, they also created an idyllic Provençal courtyard overlooking their vineyard, with everything you'd find in the South of France, except for the buzz of the cicadas. They produce six Rosé wines, and if you're already a Rosé enthusiast you'll know that this is a wine that can make the afternoon slip by

very quickly. One of the stand-outs is their "Jolie", with distinct aromas of red pepper and flavors of juniper, pine, and truffles. The wines typically sell out by the end of the summer. Prices range from $20 to $30.

RAPHAEL

39390 Route 25, Peconic
631.765.1100
www.raphaelwine.com

Raphael is the vision of John Petrocelli, who drew inspiration from his ancestral home in Italy to carry on a centuries' old winemaking tradition. John's emphasis is on the cycles of nature and winemaking with a minimalist but exacting touch, and all the harvesting at Raphael is done by hand, an increasing rarity in wine production. The winery is built twelve-feet underground to provide natural temperature regulation and to make use of the gentle gravity-flow method in winemaking, which reduces the amount of oxygen to which the wine is exposed, and the wine tours here are an education. You'll get a tour through their tank room, production facility, and winery, as well as a chance to ask all your questions. The tour is popular and can fill up quickly, so if you're keen it's best to make reservations by calling ahead to ensure a spot.

John's reds are largely Bordeaux-varietals, a mix of blends and varietal releases, and the whites are classics such as Chardonnay, Riesling, and Sauvignon Blanc. The Raphael tasting room is located on the Main Road (Route 25) in Peconic, and wines range from about $20 to $40. Summer weekends there include special live-music events and artisanal food-and-wine pairings.

BEDELL CELLARS

36225 New York State Route 25, Cutchogue
631.734.7537
www.bedellcellars.com

Founded as a small family vineyard in 1980, Bedell Cellars has since cemented its reputation as one of the premium-quality wine producers, not just in the North Fork, but anywhere in the country. When White House sommeliers had to select wines for President Obama's inaugural dinner in 2013, the Bedell Merlot was on the menu. A series of 90+ ratings along the way

didn't hurt either. Today, with case production right around 10,000, Bedell is a mid-sized family winery with an increasingly large reputation.

While many winemakers in this still emergent wine country are experimenting with styles, blends, and techniques, Bedell's winemaker, Rich Olsen-Harbich, is something of a traditionalist, whose interests are in sustainable practices and natural winemaking. He uses only native yeasts and French oak barrels, creating aroma and flavor profiles that are both honest and brilliant.

The tasting room at Bedell is a historic 1919 potato barn, with high ceilings and tastefully done interiors, and it was named one of the top twenty-five tasting rooms in America by *Wine Enthusiast* magazine. The tasting room walls are adorned with original artwork by collectible contemporary artists, and several of these commissioned pieces feature on their bottle labels.

Bedell makes about twenty different wines, mostly red and white with some sparkling, created from a meticulous blend of up to fifty small batches, fermented separately for each vintage.

You'll want to save some of these wines, such as the "Musée" Merlot, for that special dinner, but you might be tempted to finish their easy drinking and deliciously aromatic "First Crush" white on their outdoor porch. Most wines are in the $30 - $70 range, with some notable premium and cellar-worthy exceptions. The tasting room welcomes walk-ins, as do most other wineries in the area, but reservations are recommended given the popularity of Bedell.

Taste

COFFEE POT CELLARS

31855 Main Road, Cutchogue
631.765.8929
www.coffeepotcellars.com

Winemaker Adam Suprenant shares his sun-lit and cheerfully airy tasting room at Coffee Pot Cellars with the beekeeping passions of his wife, Laura. It's a charming blend of two visions. Adam got his first job in a vineyard in 1986 and started his career working in Napa and Bordeaux before starting his own label here in 2011. The idea for the name Coffee Pot Cellars came when he was striped bass

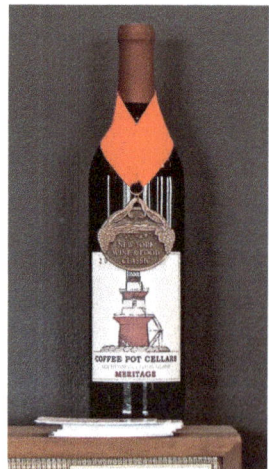

fishing off Orient Point on the easternmost tip of Long Island and was inspired by the lighthouse shaped as a coffee percolator. It's this kind of quirky local history that makes the North Fork special.

Today, Adam sources grapes from local producers to make about 750–1000 cases of his handcrafted wines, and he'll tell you that he believes in being true to the fruit and in making wines that don't use any gimmicks. His current line-up—and the plan is to remain small and specialized—includes Gewürztraminer, Cabernet Franc, a Meritage blend of Merlot, Petit Verdot, Cabernet Franc, and Cabernet Sauvignon that recently garnered high accolades from the *Wine Enthusiast.* Most wines range from $15 to $25.

WATER'S CREST

28735 Main Road, Cutchogue
631.734.5065
www.waterscrest.com

Home winemaker, turned award-winning producer, Jim Waters
is one of those people who is so unambiguously passionate
about making exceptional wines that it's hard to imagine he
ever did anything else. That, however, is not the case. Jim only
started making wine in 2001, after serving as a fireman in New
York City on 9/11. Today, Jim makes between 1,000 and 1,500
cases of some ultra-premium wines with grapes carefully selected from local growers and with some Riesling sourced from

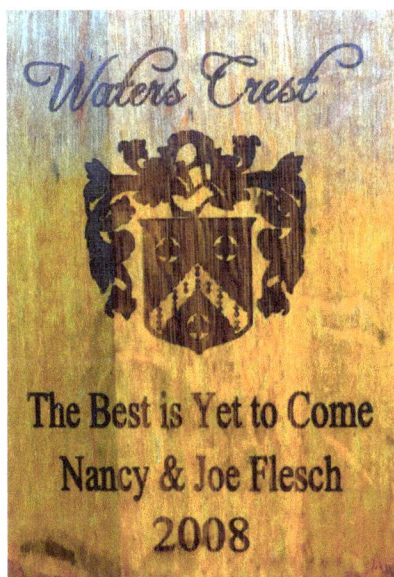

The Best is Yet to Come
Nancy & Joe Flesch
2008

upstate growers. Not bound by the restrictions that some of his European counterparts complain can hamstring them, Jim boldly experiments with winemaking styles and blends, and his success with these innovations have brought his wines to the industry's attention.

Water's Crest is what they might call on the West Coast "garage" winemaking. The tasting room here is a whole lot more warehouse than it is Tuscan palace, and frankly, that is part of the refreshing charm of Jim's operation. Here, the wine is everything. And if you want to try some wines you might otherwise not get a chance to taste, visiting Jim is a great way to do it. In a region not traditionally known for its Sauvignon Blanc wines, he ages his for two months in French oak. He also makes a wine he calls Campania Rosso, a Merlot-Cabernet Franc blend named after the region in Italy where Jim's ancestors started making wine and a part of the family still does, as well as a limited-production Alsatian-style dry Riesling with a leisurely finish. Jim can often be found in the winery or tasting room and welcomes visitors to witness the winemaking operations. The tasting room is open from Friday to Monday.

McCALL WINES

22600 New York State Route 25, Cutchogue
631.734.5764
www.mccallwines.com

The vineyards at McCall Wines grow today on a piece of land with a long history. Until about three hundred years ago, the land was the cultural center of the Algonquin tribe and was known by settlers as Fort Corchaug. For this reason, the vineyard that Russell McCall planted here in 1997 was originally called Corchaug Estate Vineyard, in recognition of this history. And although the McCalls have been growing grapes here since the 1990s, they didn't want to put their own name on a bottle until they were convinced that the wine would be excellent. It was only in 2007 that they released their first vintage.

The McCalls believe in doing only a few things and doing them well. Given this philosophy, the focus here is mainly on Pinot Noir and Merlot, although they do make some Chardonnay and Sauvignon Blanc. If you are a Pinot Noir fan, you will want to make a leisurely stop at McCall especially. The finicky, thin-skinned, delicate Pinot Noir grape is difficult to grow even in the best of climates, which gives it its nickname: the heartbreak grape. Growing it in the marginal climate of the North Fork is a sheer act of courage. The Pinot Noir grown here are originally

French clones, sourced from growers in Oregon's famed Willamette Valley.

The high-ceilinged tasting room is located in a reclaimed barn and retains a distinctive old-world charm. There is also plenty of wildlife to be spotted on the adjacent farm – especially foxes, pheasants, and turtles. McCall was named New York Wine and Grape Foundation's "Winery of the Year" in 2013, and most wines range from $18 to $40, although the Pinot Noir reserve is upward of $75.

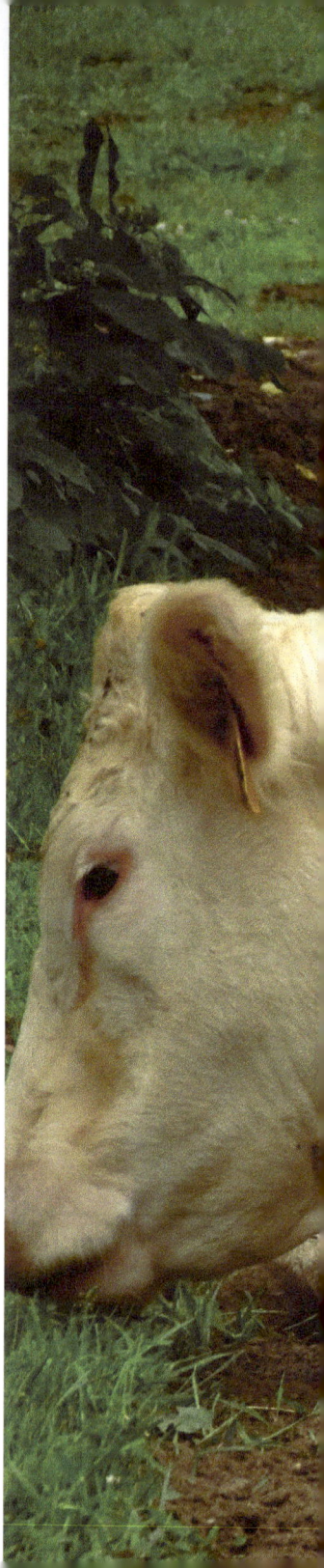

JAMESPORT VINEYARDS

1216 Main Road, Jamesport
631.722.5256
www.jamesportwines.com

Founded in 1981, when Ron and Ann Marie Goerler bought a farm in Cutchogue that they had long admired, Jamesport Vineyards is one of the North Fork's oldest wineries. The family eventually bought the 1850s wood-shingled barn that houses the winery and tasting room as well, and, since its inception, Jamesport has been a father-son operation. Today, three generations of the Goerler family are involved in winemaking. The family think of themselves as stewards of the land and are dedicated to sustainable viticulture.

Today, they produce about 4,000 cases, only using fruit grown on their sixty acres of land, making this a fully estate winery, and they are quietly forging a reputation for Cabernet Franc. They have won best in class in the New York State competitions in the past, sometimes for years running. Most wines are in the $15 to $40 price range, with just a few hundred cases produced of the higher-end wines.

PAUMANOK VINEYARDS

1074 Main Road, Aquebogue
631.722.8800
www.paumanok.com

Ursula and Charles Massoud were living in Kuwait when the
idea of making their own wine first crossed their minds as
a distant retirement dream. It was 1971 and finding wine in
Kuwait was next to impossible. Pining for a glass of Riesling,
it occurred to them that, in order to find a bottle, they might
have to make it themselves. While visiting friends in the United
States a few years later, they saw a newspaper article about
the fledgling Long Island wine scene. Soon, they were active-
ly hunting for a vineyard land acquisition. It was the early
1980s, and farm land in this area was not yet at the premium it
commands today. The region was just beginning to make good
quality wine, and there were only a handful of producers. They
settled on a forty-two acre plot of land in Aquebogue. There,
Charles and Ursula started by planting varieties they liked to
drink and those they thought would do well here – Chardonnay, Riesling, Merlot and Cabernet Franc. Later they brought in
additional plantings of Chenin Blanc and Petit Verdot.

Today, after more than three decades in operation, the winery has become an intergenerational family business. Their three sons all have active roles in the business.

Paumanok, drawing the inspiration for its name from the Native American word for Long Island, is one of the first wineries to grow Chenin Blanc in the region, and it is their flagship varietal. Their Chenin Blanc has won praise from *The New York Times'* Eric Asimov, and *Wine Advocate* has awarded several 90+ ratings to Paumanok wines. They were also named the New York State winery of the year in 2015. Most wines range from $15 to $50.

ROANOKE VINEYARDS

3543 Sound Avenue, Riverhead
Second tasting room in Mattituck at 165 Love Lane, Mattituck
631.727.4161
www.roanokevineyards.net

The story of Roanoke's octogenarian vineyard master, Gabby Pisacano, and his experiment with the 2007 vintage, is a classic North Fork wine-country story. Back in 2007, when Gabby first talked about thinning the fruit clusters dramatically to get better maritime air circulation and sunlight, even his own team thought he was a bit crazy. It didn't make sense to drop that much fruit, not in this climate. That year, he was given just twelve rows of Cabernet Franc to carry out his vineyard experiment.

That year, just 172 cases of wine were produced from Gabby's part of the vineyard, and when the fruit rolled in at harvest the folks at Roanoke quickly realized that they were looking at grapes with superlative complexity, and structure. Samples of the wine were sent to the legendary wine critic Robert Parker on a lark, and the wine got a 91-point score from the tastemaker. *The New York Times* proclaimed that Roanoke had "mastered Cabernet Franc," and the 2008 vintage has Gabby's portrait on the label.

Today, the production has gone up to a couple of thousand cases, although the wine often sells out quickly and purchases are limited. Sometimes, the tasting room is your only chance to get a sample. Fortunately, the tasting room is a delightful place to spend an hour or two, and, weather permitting, the outdoor tables in the back are a perfect chance to enjoy what is very likely the best Cabernet Franc this region has to offer on an even more leisurely schedule. You might even catch a glimpse of Gabby inspecting the vineyard.

T'JARA VINEYARDS

917.497.3073
www.tjaravineyards.com

T'Jara is what happens when two friends share a passion for wine, for business, and for the North Fork wine region. Russell and Jed met in 1990 while working for La Reve winery in Southampton, and both men harbored a dream of one day making their own wine from grapes they grew themselves. Russell had over thirty years of experience as a winemaker in several countries around the globe, and today he's still the Long Island winemaker with the most 90+ scores from *Wine Spectator*. Jed had decades of experience in marketing in the wine world. The duo teamed up in 2000 and, in what they admit might have been putting the cart before the horse, actually bought rootstock before they had land to grow it on. Their first limited release came in 2005, from blended samples, and soon T'Jara was born.

T'Jara does not have a tasting room yet, but their wines can be sampled at three wine-tasting collectives in the region: the Winemaking Studio in Peconic, the Empire Cellars tasting room in Riverhead, and at Brooklyn Oenology in New York City. Their wines are also on a number of prestigious wine lists in the city. With only three wines in their program—usually a

Merlot, a Cabernet Franc, and a reserve wine from a changing varietal—this is as small-batch and handcrafted as it gets. Most wines are around $25, and they plan to eventually produce about 3,000 cases of wine.

SHINN ESTATE VINEYARDS AND FARMHOUSE

2000 Oregon Road, Mattituck
631.804.0367
www.shinnestatevineyards.com

Barbara Shinn and David Page, the proprietors at Shinn Estate Vineyards, first met in 1988, in the San Francisco Bay Area, and moved to New York a few years later to open the East Coast's first farm-to-table restaurant, Home. This was before farm-to-table restaurants were in vogue, and the city quickly embraced the Pages. In 2001, they wrote a cookbook *Recipes from Home,* which went on to become something of a phenomenon and attracted a fair bit of attention. When they decided to purchase twenty acres of land in the North Fork and start an estate winery, few who knew Barbara and David were surprised when, within just a few years, their wines were being lauded as some of the best in New York State. Strong believers in sustainable and biodynamic vineyard practices, their wines reflect a deep and uncompromising connection to the land, and Barbara's guided vineyard walks on weekends are highly recommended if you have an interest in viticulture.

The Shinn tasting room is located on Oregon Road in Mattituck, just a mile north of Route 48. Their wines are also poured in a wide selection of New York City and Long Island restaurants. Most wines are in the $15 to $40 price range.

LIEB CELLARS

13050 Oregon Road, Cutchogue
631.734.1100
www.liebcellars.com

Russell Hearn, the Australian-born winemaker at Lieb Cellars, has over three decades of winemaking experience. With fruit grown using sustainable farming practices from hand-tended vines, some of which are the oldest in the North Fork, Russell makes a range of excellent wines. Some of the reserve wines, such as the Meritage, have great aging potential and are made using low-yield farming techniques, with Lieb Cellars sometimes picking only one grape cluster per shoot. Their Pinot Blanc and Blanc de Blancs sparkling wines have gained national recognition.

Lieb started as a small estate in 1992 and since then has grown both in popularity and size, but still remains true to its roots. In 2004, they started the Bridge Lane series, which are lighter, easy-drinking, "everyday" wines at more approachable price points. They now have two tasting rooms – the first one is just north of Sound Ave in Mattituck and a second, more rustic tasting room is located on a rural road in Cutchogue on Oregon Road. The Oregon road site is our favorite for charm. It is distinctly back-lane and does not allow buses, large limos, or

·173·

groups larger than eight. The outdoor patio offers views of the vineyards, and they host regular live music events.

ONE WOMAN WINES AND VINEYARDS

5195 Old North Road, Southold
631.765.1200
www.onewomanwines.com

From the wrap-around porch on Claudia Purita's beach-style tasting room, you can generally see two things in summer: the carefully tended vines, laden with ripening fruit, and Claudia out there on her tractor. Claudia grew up on her family's farm in Calabria, Italy, and developed a love for the land as a girl. As the name of her winery suggests, this vineyard is largely the result of her labor and dedication to producing high-quality wines and that abiding passion. Most of the vineyard work is done by hand, from planting to pruning and picking, and, although it's still technically a one-woman endeavor, you will often find Claudia's daughter, Gabriella, pouring in the tasting room.

Claudia's focus is on aromatic white wines, especially Gewürz-traminer and Grüner Veltliners. She also makes a Sancerre-style Sauvignon Blanc and some excellent creamy Chardonnays. The only red wines she makes are two versions of Merlot – a regular one and an estate reserve merlot, both fermented in French oak and both with intense and excellent values.

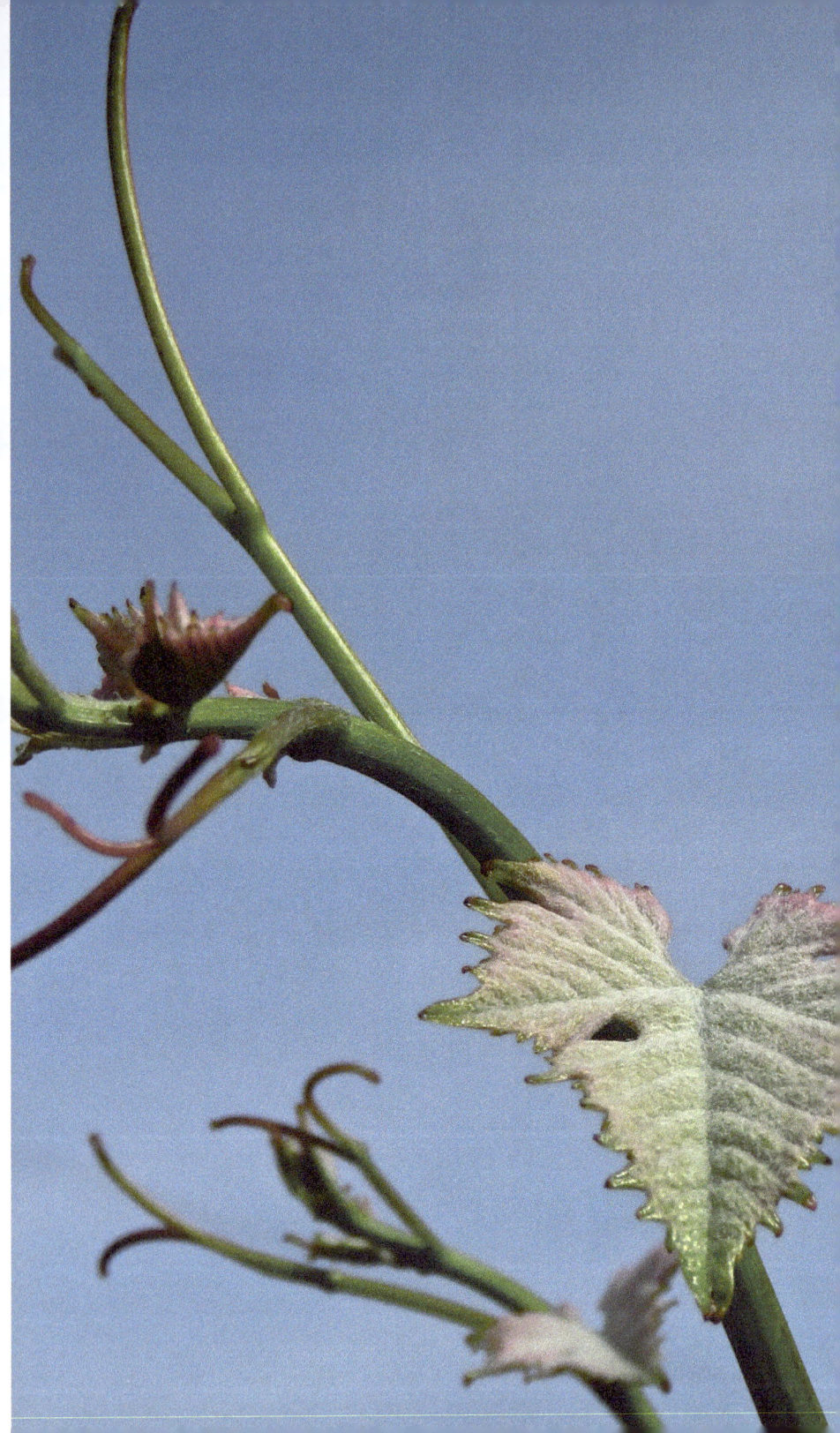

If you're in the area on the weekend, check out Claudia's Saturday night event – "Tasting Under the Stars" – which has been going strong for more than five years now. There's a roaring bonfire, outdoor movies, s'mores, and even a telescope for taking a peek at the night sky *al fresco*. There is no better spot in the North Fork for sipping your wine under a starlit sky.

CHANNING DAUGHTERS

1927 Scuttle Hole Road, Bridgehampton
631.537.7224
www.channingdaughters.com

While the North Fork of Long Island has the lion's share of wineries and gets most of the attention, the "South Fork," more popularly known as "The Hamptons," has its own AVA, with distinctly different soil types and microclimates.

Chris Tracy is the winemaker at Channing Daughters, and his passion for making a range of interesting and innovative whites have earned the estate a reputation as one of the top Long Island wineries, along with a good deal of media attention and some high-flying accolades. Chris is also a chef and certified sommelier, and these are wines, perhaps not surprisingly, that are food friendly. He makes wines from over two-dozen grape varietals, some of which are unique grape species not grown by many other producers in the area, such as Teroldego, Refosco, and Lagrein. About half of their fruit is grown on the twenty-eight acres of estate vineyards, while the other half is carefully selected from other growers in the area, with fruit coming from all three Long Island AVAs – North Fork, the Hamptons, and Long Island.

Channing Daughters is best known for its portfolio of Rosé wines, ranging widely in color, complexity, and taste. And, even though they make a total of about 14,000 cases annually, which make them a relatively large winery in the area, everything in the winemaking process is done in small batches here. Most wines range from $18 to $40, and there is a wide variety to choose from, to suit a range of interests.

Eating

NOAH'S

136 Front Street, Greenport
631.477.6720
www.chefnoahs.com

Chef Noah Schwartz's restaurant, in the heart of Greenport, serves locally sourced, seasonal, and seafood-centered eclectic fare. The small-plate menu ensures that you get to try a range of creations. Zagat describes their fish-focused dishes as "flat out off the hook," and, while the menu changes often, local favorites are the red crab tacos and duck BBQ.

The local wine selection is one of the widest in the area, and, for a restaurant located in a wine producing region, they make exceptionally good cocktails, in case you are in need of a break from grapes. It can get busy on summer weekends and reservations are highly recommended.

THE FRISKY OYSTER

27 Front Street, Greenport
631.477.4265
www.thefriskyoyster.com

When the Frisky Oyster opened in 2002, the dining scene in the North Fork was still very casual and the area was a long way off from becoming a dining destination. That has now changed, of course, and the Frisky Oyster retains its status as *the* go-to place to satisfy your oyster cravings. The red wallpapered interior and the vibe on most nights is downtown Manhattan-chic meets wine country. The Oysters Friskafella is a signature dish, along with the Crescent Farms duck breast with creamy polenta. On a warm summer evening, the outdoor tables offer a great view on Front Street to watch the world go by. Reservations are recommended.

LOVE LANE KITCHEN

240 Love Lane, Mattituck
631.298.8989
www.lovelanekitchen.com

Love Lane Kitchen in Mattituck is open for breakfast, lunch, and dinner. In fact, they serve breakfast till 2 p.m. – perfect for that late, late morning brunch you meant to get out of bed for sooner. With its unpretentious and light-filled interior, it is popular with locals and tourists alike. Their outdoor garden table is perfect for an *al fresco* dining experience, weather permitting.

CUTCHOGUE DINER

27800 Main Road, Cutchogue
631.734.7016
www.cutchoguediner.com

This authentic 1941 diner is a North Fork landmark, with its vintage lighting fixtures and marble countertop. Open until 3 pm, this is the perfect spot to start your day or to refuel for the second-half of a heavy wine tasting afternoon. Apart from the usual diner fare, there's enough here to keep vegetarians happy too - try the mushroom burger or the pancakes. Their home-made pies (a la mode, of course) are highly recommended.

PROVISIONS AND INGREDIENTS

2885 Peconic Lane, Peconic
774.641.7488
www.anthonynappawines.com/provisions.html

Located next door to the Winemaker Studio in Peconic, this is Chef Sarah Evans' project. She sells a curated collection of cured Italian meats, local cheeses, dried foods and local wine—in short, everything that you need for a gastronomic wine-country picnic. Alternatively, you may just want to park yourself at the outdoor tables and sample Sarah's delectable sandwiches.

FIRST AND SOUTH

100 South Street, Greenport
631.333.2200
www.firstandsouth.com

This is the venture of Chef Taylor Knapp, who worked under Rene Redzepi at Noma in Copenhagen, a Michelin two-star place regularly named as the best restaurant in the world. The cuisine at First and South can best be described as inventive and quirky, with dishes that look as good as they taste. The new American-style menu features some traditional favorites, such as the South Street Chowder and a really good burger, described on the menu as, well, "A Really Good Burger." This is world-class home cooking. If you're in town Tuesday through Friday, don't miss the four-course *prix fixe* menu for around $40.

LAVENDER BY THE BAY

7540 New York State Route 25, East Marion
631.477.1019
www.lavenderbythebay.com

Driving on the main road through East Marion, if you see a sea of purple on the side of the road, it is time for a detour. Lavender by the Bay is one of the largest lavender farms in the United States and welcomes tourists seven days a week from June through September. You can explore over twenty varieties of lavender planted on over seventeen acres. They offer freshly cut bunches, lavender plants, dried lavender sachets, and honey from their own beehives. This is a great photo-op location if you want to memorialize your back-lane adventures.

ORIENT BEACH STATE PARK

40000 Main Road, Orient
631.323.2440

Located at the tip of the North Fork, in the town of Southold, this state park is home to Long Beach, a designated National Natural Landmark. The ecosystem ranges from a salt marsh to a maritime red cedar forest, with the attendant diverse variety of flora and fauna. For bird-watchers, this is the place to spot ospreys and diamondbacks. But for the rest of us, the park has picnic tables and trails for hiking and biking over its more than 350 acres. Best of all, the Orient Long Beach Bar Light—a lighthouse off the town of Orient, commonly known as Bug Light, and not a cocktail spot—is located inside the park. The park is open throughout the year.

SHELTER ISLAND

Take the ferry from Greenport to Shelter Island to enter a world that feels equal parts south of France, Martha's Vineyard, and Long Island *circa* 1975. Cars and bikes are both allowed on the eight-minute ferry trip, but the limited number of shops and restaurants helps to preserve this tiny island's unblemished rural charm. Driving around, you will very likely come across small, isolated beaches that seem untouched. And that's because, for the most part, they are.

Shelter Island has a rich and storied past, with its colonial history dating back to 1620, when it was included in a land grant made by James I of England. In the following decades, the island changed hands many times before being sold to a group of Barbados sugar merchants for 1600 pounds of sugar in 1651. Nathaniel Sylvester, one of those merchants, was the island's first white settler. One of the manor houses built by the Sylvester family still stands today, located just off of New York State Route 114.

NOTES

_____
_____
_____
_____
_____
_____
_____
_____
_____
_____
_____
_____
_____
_____
_____
_____
_____
_____

NOTES

_____

_____

_____

_____

_____

_____

_____

_____

_____

_____

_____

_____

_____

_____

_____

_____

_____

_____

NOTES

_____

_____

_____

_____

_____

_____

_____

_____

_____

_____

_____

_____

_____

_____

_____

_____

_____

NOTES

NOTES

_____

_____

_____

_____

_____

_____

_____

_____

_____

_____

_____

_____

_____

_____

_____

_____

_____

_____

NOTES

NOTES

NOTES

NOTES

NOTES

NOTES

_____
_____
_____
_____
_____
_____
_____
_____
_____
_____
_____
_____
_____
_____
_____
_____
_____
_____
_____

INDEX

ABOUT THE AUTHORS

NISH GERA IS A WRITER AND FILMMAKER CURRENTLY based in Brussels, Belgium. His writing appears regularly in the Huffington Post. The Back Lane Wineries of New York State is his first book.

TILAR J. MAZZEO IS THE NEW YORK TIMES BESTSELLing author of The Widow Clicquot: The Story of a Champagne Empire and an established wine writer, whose other works include The Back Lane Wineries of Napa and The Back Lane Wineries of Sonoma. Her wine writing has appeared in venues including Food & Wine, Mental Floss, and other national outlets across the US. She is the proprietor and winemaker at Parsell Vineyard, in Saanichton, British Columbia, on Canada's Vancouver Island.

ABOUT THE PHOTOGRAPHER

PETER VERBRUGGHE IS A BELGIAN DIPLOMAT, WHO moonlights as a photographer and wine enthusiast. His highly attuned nose has had many a winemaker reach for a pen and paper to update their wine notes with the subtle aromas that had remained undetected.

www.ingramcontent.com/pod-product-compliance
Lightning Source LLC
Chambersburg PA
CBHW051210090426
42740CB00022B/3454